THE MARCH OF THE INSTITUTIONS

'I call upon each and every Hand of the Cause of God . . . upon the entire body of the believers . . . and upon their elected representatives . . . to meet the challenge, and seize the opportunities . . . of accelerating the march of the institutions of His world-redeeming Order, and of hastening the establishment of His Kingdom in the hearts of men.'

Shoghi Effendi's last words addressed to the Bahá'ís of the world, October 1957

THE MARCH OF THE INSTITUTIONS

*A Commentary on the Interdependence
of Rulers and Learned*

by

EUNICE BRAUN

GEORGE RONALD

OXFORD

By the same author

FROM STRENGTH TO STRENGTH
A CROWN OF BEAUTY

GEORGE RONALD, Publisher
46 High Street, Kidlington, Oxford OX5 2DN

ISBN 0-85398-182-5 Hardcover
ISBN 0-85398-183-3 Softcover

Printed in England by Billing & Sons Ltd, Worcester

Contents

To Leonard

with deepest love and gratitude

Acknowledgments

Acknowledgment is made to the Board of Counselors in the Americas and especially to Mrs Velma Sherrill of St Louis, Missouri, who conceived the idea for this book and gave encouragement for its writing; and to those members of the International Teaching Center who were kind enough to read the manuscript in an earlier, briefer version and offer recommendations as well as encouragement for its publication.

Appreciation is extended to May Hofman Ballerio for her effective editorial assistance, and to Russell Busey, long-time publishing colleague and friend, for encouragement and advice. Thanks are also expressed to those individuals, named in the content of the text, who have permitted the author to quote from their spoken words: Dhikru'lláh Khádem, Hand of the Cause of God; Hushmand Fatheazam and 'Alí Nakhjavání, members of the Universal House of Justice; Edna True, former member of the North American Board of Counselors and of the National Spiritual Assembly of the USA; Dr Jalil Mahmoudi, Auxiliary Board Member in America; and to Dr. Jane Faily, member of the National Spiritual Assembly of Canada, for graciously providing the accompanying Foreword.

Glenview, Illinois   Eunice Braun
Riḍván, 1984

Foreword

This book needed to be written. It presents clearly the essential characteristics of Bahá'u'lláh's Administrative Order, enabling both the enquirer and the avowed supporter to appreciate the features of a system designed by a Messenger of God to accomplish the unification of mankind. That system, which claims to possess the capacity to order human affairs in a time when the inadequacy of other structures threatens to annihilate human life, deserves thoughtful attention.

As the Bahá'í goal of planetary unity is unique in the history of religions, so are the structures and processes which define Bahá'í administration unique in the history of past systems. In this divine system the positive elements of past governmental organization have been preserved and their fatal deficiencies amended. Preserved within the Bahá'í design are the greatness of monarchy, the excellence of aristocracy, and the vitality of democracy; absent are the risks of despotism, aloofness, or mob rule. Here is a religious system free from rigidity, possessed of sufficient power and authority to maintain peace among nations, and yet a channel of compassion which tenderly nourishes individual growth.

Power is needed to order human affairs; the struggle for power threatens to destroy human society. The resolution of this paradox is the signal achievement of Bahá'í administration. One example exists in the process of consultation; this unique method for searching out truth and resolving conflict permeates the entire Bahá'í system. In consultation each individual is challenged to reach the highest development of his own potential in the very process of serving the interests of the common weal.

There are two branches of Bahá'í institutions: one, called the 'rulers', is comprised of bodies exercising authority; the other, called the 'learned', is comprised of individuals who possess knowledge. In the relationship between them is born an organic process which frees mankind from tyranny by the power of either branch alone. The age-old dream of a philosopher king is realized. Resolution of paradox sings out from the marvelous interdependence prescribed for the 'rulers' and the 'learned' in the Bahá'í system. Bahá'u'lláh wrote to the kings advising them to appoint wise and honest counselors. In His own system He provided for the 'rulers', wielders of authority, exactly such independent and sagacious advisors. Thus the blindness of power, and its arrogance, is dissolved through consultation with the wise and visionary 'learned'. And the 'learned' are guarded against their own form of tyranny, the practice of aloof criticism, or of sedition itself. They must offer their wisdom, like nourishing milk, to both the 'rulers' and the growing body politic. From such precise balancing of elements the grace and vitality of divine creation springs forth.

The entrancing magic of this dualism calls to mind the interplay between justice and mercy, male and female, right lobe and left lobe, upon whose harmonious dialog depends balance in society, the creation of new human life, and human consciousness itself. Such organic resolution of elements which have formerly devolved into destructive power struggles wrecking religious systems, governments, families, and individual psyches, is the hallmark of the Bahá'í system.

The March of the Institutions depicts the structures and processes of this organic spiritual system and meets the needs of different readers. To those new to the subject it delineates a system which reflects the greatness of its Origin, making it possible to see that organized religion may be a creative rather than a destructive force in our time. To Bahá'ís, laboring mightily to upraise these institutions, it reveals the greatness of their task; the matchless beauty of the Beloved is glimpsed through the delicate and majestic balance of His wondrous system. To those serving within the institutions of the 'rulers' and the 'learned' it is a beckoning call to set aside the habits of power struggle, and to seize our partner and dance to the melody of the Nightingale of God.

A. Jane Faily
Naw-Rúz, 1984

Introduction

Throughout the history of organized society, religious communities — in their endeavour to build the 'City of God' on earth — have striven to maintain their unity, to establish a balance between the spirit and the form and to avoid the schismatic forces that have nevertheless repeatedly rent them asunder. These forces have evoked violence and war, within and without, the very antipathy of the peaceful, unifying purpose of their Founders. Christianity itself did not escape this fragmentation — indeed, it offers a prime example. Perhaps this was partially due to the once fervent commitment to establishing the Kingdom of God 'on earth as it is in heaven'. That this was predicated upon the return of Christ, the 'Spirit of Truth', the Son of Man 'come in the glory (or station) of the Father', was overlooked and largely forgotten.

Many difficulties were due to the fact that the governing and legislative authority on the one hand, and spiritual guidance and inspiration on the other, were both invested in individuals, the 'divines': priests, ministers, bishops, doctors of religious law. Power and authority residing too heavily in individuals inevitably leads to differences of opinion, to the formation of a following and to the shattering of the community.

Bahá'u'lláh has established through His Revelation a new and unique system of checks and balances which for the first time in religious history eliminates this age-old problem. He has created the form through which alone the spirit of His teachings flow. He has preordained institutions that clearly establish the perimeters within which both the 'rulers' and 'learned' (the two arms of His Administrative Order) carry out their separate functions, yet meet and are one.

'The newness and uniqueness of this concept make it difficult to grasp,' the Universal House of Justice has stated, and 'only as the Bahá'í Community grows and the believers are increasingly able to contemplate its administrative structure uninfluenced by concepts from past ages, will the vital interdependence of the "rulers" and "learned" in the Faith be properly understood, and the inestimable value of their interaction be fully recognized.'[1]

One arm of this order, under the generic term of 'rulers', encompasses the corporate, elected bodies known presently as Local and National Spiritual Assemblies. They govern, direct and administer the affairs of the community on both local and national levels.

The other arm is composed of the Hands of the Cause of God, the Boards of Counselors and the Auxiliary Board members and their assistants — all of these institutions coming under the umbrella of the 'learned', and all appointed to their functions, not elected.

The Supreme Body, the Universal House of Justice, also a corporate, elected, ruling body on the international level, stands sovereign over all. At its side, seated in the Holy Land, is posited the International Teaching Center, composed of all the Hands of the Cause of God, with a working nucleus of Hands and Counselors at the World Center, serving and aiding the Supreme Body. It is the seal and crown of the institution of the learned, coordinating the work of all the Boards of Counselors throughout the world, and serving as a right arm to the Universal House of Justice.

'Blessed are the rulers and the learned among the people of Bahá. They are my trustees among My servants and the manifestation of My commandments amidst My people,' Bahá'u'lláh reveals in the Book of His Covenant, the *Kitáb-i-'Ahd.*

There exist in the Bahá'í Faith certain distinguishing terms and titles which can only be understood and defined within the context of the Faith itself. Among these are such terms as: Hands of the Cause of God; the Universal House of Justice; Spiritual Assemblies; and also the term 'rulers and learned' which Bahá'u'lláh used as the all-over generic term to define the two lines of administrative authority and responsibility of His Faith. These terms have therefore only vague and indefinite meaning to one who is not familiar with the Bahá'í Faith and its institutions, nor can they be understood within the confines of everyday experience. Thus the term 'rulers', which brings to mind the thought of presidents, emperors and kings, means instead the corporate, elected bodies mentioned above wherein no one person has more authority than another.

The term 'learned' does not necessarily designate academic and scholastic ability or worldly achievements — though any and all such human accomplishments may very well apply to a given individual appointed to such a position of responsibility in the Faith. It is rather in a spiritual context that the term must be understood, and frequently 'Abdu'l-Bahá, in defining the qualities needed for those appointed to this function, speaks of the 'spiritually learned'. These are also qualities which every teacher of the Cause is called upon to attain in order to be effective in teaching the Faith. The difference is that the Hand of the Cause, Counselor, or Board member has certain specific functions and responsibilities toward the Bahá'í community that are ongoing and continuous — responsibilities that rest upon that individual at all times in respect to the believers served.

Moreover, while 'Abdu'l-Bahá states in *The Secret of Divine Civilization* that 'the spiritually learned must be characterized by both inward and outward perfections . . . a good character, an enlightened nature . . . temperance, reverence, and a heartfelt fear of God . . .' these are also, stated in various ways, among the requisites for those who serve on Spiritual Assemblies, where the views of many become submerged and blended into one view.

The following chapters attempt to explore 'the march of the institutions', to use Shoghi Effendi's term; especially the comparatively recent rise and meteoric development of the institution of the 'learned', and more particularly the 'vital interdependence' of the 'rulers' and 'learned' in the Faith.

1

'With Neither Peer nor Likeness'

The Spiritual Assembly — A Divine Institution

The purpose and functions of Spiritual Assemblies, who serve the Bahá'í community as corporate, elected administrative bodies, have been within the experience of Bahá'ís for more than eighty years. Even before His release from prison in 1908, 'Abdu'l-Bahá had addressed numerous tablets to Spiritual Assemblies in various cities in both East and West. In 1903, only ten years following the first mention of the Faith of Bahá'u'lláh in America at the Columbian Exposition in Chicago, 'Abdu'l-Bahá had already addressed a message to the Chicago Assembly concerning the raising of a Bahá'í Temple in America. Even to contemplate such a formidable task today, for *any* Local Spiritual Assembly, would be staggering, buttressed though we are with thirty-six years of detailed guidance from Shoghi Effendi, supported by a National Spiritual Assembly and sheltered within the stronghold of the Universal House of Justice.

Perhaps it is true, as we sometimes say with facile assurance, knowing so little of the reality of life and times in that day, that those early Assemblies had little concept of the essential nature of their being or of their future structure. They did not know the pattern by which the Administrative Order of the Faith would evolve; nor could they conceive at that time of their inherent position as foundation stones in the raising of a Divine Economy: the World Order of Bahá'u'lláh. What they did possess to high degree was absolute faith in the Revelation of Bahá'u'lláh and in the guidance of 'Abdu'l-Bahá, little as they yet possessed of the printed Word. World vision the Master gave them from the beginning. They accepted wholeheartedly His assurance that through these Spiritual Assemblies 'the lights of knowledge are shed abroad over all things'; that one day the whole world would be 'one native land, its diverse peoples one single kind, the nations of both east and west one household'.[2]

Few letters sent forth by the Master contain more joy, hope and promise than those He sent to these first Spiritual Assemblies as they were formed, divine institutions 'with neither peer nor likeness in the cycles gone before'.* Today, standing some eighty years farther along the road of destiny, with over 30,000 Spiritual Assemblies spread throughout the planet, our comprehension of the World Order of Bahá'u'lláh, functioning in that future golden age, is still a matter of seeing 'through a glass darkly'.

'Who is it', Shoghi Effendi has written, 'that can imagine the lofty standard which such a civilization, as it unfolds itself, is destined to attain?'[3]

Nevertheless, with a few broad brushstrokes upon the horizon of history, he has given us glimpses of the glory and wonder of that day which the Bahá'ís of our time are

---

* Selections from the Writings of 'Abdu'l-Bahá, p. 78.

helping to shape: 'Then will a world civilization be born, flourish, and perpetuate itself, a civilization with a fullness of life such as the world has never seen nor can as yet conceive . . . Then will the promise enshrined in all the Books of God be redeemed, and all the prophecies uttered by the Prophets of old come to pass, and the vision of seers and poets be realized.'[4] And from time to time the Universal House of Justice has lifted our sights above our daily tasks toward 'the broad uplands of the Most Great Peace'.

The Essential Priorities of a Spiritual Assembly

In an informal talk given in Wilmette, Hushmand Fatheazam, member of the Universal House of Justice, told the assembled Bahá'ís that today is not the day for achieving perfection in the Administrative Order. 'This edifice of the World Order of Bahá'u'lláh is so big . . . time will give us a better perspective of this Divine majestic edifice . . .'

Establishing a spirit of unity amongst the members of the Assembly and the believers is essential, and this comes about through teaching. 'The purpose of every Spiritual Assembly is to be a purified spirit for teaching the Cause of God', he said. 'Please do not forget what the beloved Guardian said, that the purpose of this administration is to teach the Cause of God.' And again, 'The spirit of the Faith is more important than anything else on a Spiritual Assembly.'

Unity amongst the believers and teaching the Cause of God — these are essentially the priorities given by the Master, the Guardian, and to which the Universal House of Justice is calling us today.

Unity itself encompasses and enshrines all the divine virtues. And living a Bahá'í life wherein those virtues are practised and developed becomes the chief cornerstone for teaching the Faith. Thus are both the collective and individual purposes of God for man served!

The Prime Requisites

Bahá'í consultation is the prime instrument for the successful functioning of the administrative institutions of the Faith. It is an instrument that requires continual effort: polishing, honing, fine-tuning. The Universal House of Justice speaks of the 'wonderful skill of Bahá'í consultation', that is today 'tracing new paths of human corporate action'. They also state it is 'no easy skill to learn, requiring as it does the subjugation of all egotism and unruly passions, the cultivation of frankness and freedom of thought as well as courtesy, openness of mind, and wholehearted acquiescence in a majority decision'.[5]

These are not qualities that easily and naturally accrue in a competitive and egocentric society. 'In contrast to the organizations of the world', said Edna True, 'the success and progress of the Bahá'í administrative system is through the spiritual growth and development of those who are responsible for the actual functioning of its institutions.'[6] She was speaking as a North American Counselor at the Oceanic Conference in Iceland in September 1971.

In His endeavor to educate the believers in respect to the unique nature of these divine institutions, 'Abdu'l-Bahá repeatedly stressed the spiritual virtues, the 'prime requisites for them that take counsel together'. They included 'purity of motive, radiance of spirit, detachment from all else save God, attraction to His Divine Fragrances, humility and lowliness amongst His loved ones, patience and long-suffering in difficulties and servitude to His exalted Threshold'. 'The first condition is absolute love and harmony amongst the members of the assembly . . .'[7]

Prayer is essential. How else can the aid of the Holy Spirit be attracted? They must 'turn their faces to the Kingdom on High and ask aid from the Realm of Glory . . . then proceed with the utmost devotion, courtesy, dignity, care and moderation to express their views . . . search out the truth and not insist upon their own opinion, for stubbornness and persistence in one's views will lead ultimately to discord and wrangling and the truth will remain hidden . . . it is in no wise permissible for one to belittle the thought of another . . .'[8]

Ill-feeling and discord can be avoided if 'every member expresseth with absolute freedom his own opinion . . . should anyone oppose, he must on no account feel hurt for not until matters are fully discussed can the right way be revealed'.[9]

Sometimes an assembly member will hold back his thought or opinion out of fear of being rebuffed, or pride that his ideas may not be accepted. This is as detrimental to true consultation as being overly forceful in projecting one's views on others. Neither method leads to 'searching out the truth' or arriving at a unified decision. This is not achieved by casual, passive effort, for the 'shining spark of truth cometh forth only after the clash of differing opinions'. A unified decision is not the *beginning* of consultation, but the *end* result, though assuredly consultation must proceed with harmony and the exercise of 'courtesy, dignity, moderation'.[10]

During the years when the above advice and counsel was being given by 'Abdu'l-Bahá, thereby establishing a permanent, spiritual base for Assembly functioning, the sole structure of the Administrative Order was composed of a scattering of Local Assemblies around the world guided and protected by the Master in the Holy Land. No National Assemblies, or Secondary Houses of Justice, as the Master names them in His Will and Testament, had yet evolved. When they began to emerge a few years after Shoghi Effendi was established as Guardian, it became apparent that the same spiritual qualities, conditions and requisites were essential to their able functioning.

Shoghi Effendi has summed up in a few words the secret of how the individual member can happily and success-fully function on a Spiritual Assembly: '. . . when they are called upon to arrive at a certain decision, they should, after *dispassionate, anxious,* and *cordial* consultation, turn to God in prayer, and with *earnestness* and *conviction* and *courage* record their vote and abide by the voice of the majority . . .'[11]*

To be *dispassionate* is to have that objectivity necessary to see the value of other opinions and to avoid emotional attachment to one's own. If one is *anxious*, one will cert-ainly 'search out the truth' and not take the responsibility casually or leave it to others. And if there is *cordiality* there will be an atmosphere of 'love and harmony'. Finally, having brought these conditions to bear upon the consul-tation, the members can confidently cast their votes and

italics added

make their decision with *earnestness, conviction,* and *courage.*

To know the true course and then to carry it out in action is ever the challenge to the soul treading the path of service. Shoghi Effendi, our 'true brother', understood this full well and said: 'If we but turn our gaze to the high qualifications of the members of Bahá'í Assemblies . . . we are filled with feelings of unworthiness and dismay, and would feel truly disheartened but for the comforting thought that if we rise to play nobly our part every deficiency in our lives will be more than compensated by the all-conquering spirit of His grace and power.'[12]

It is a deep privilege to serve on a Spiritual Assembly: to place oneself in that moving stream of the Administrative Order ordained by Bahá'u'lláh; to be a part of the vital process by which God is transforming the world of humanity, and through that service to transform oneself. It is an unmatchable opportunity — indeed imperative if one is called to this service — for spiritual growth and development. As the world community of believers continually expands, so do the institutions evolve to take on new requirements, challenging the individual members to stretch mind and spirit to encompass those needs.

Understanding the Bahá'í Electoral Process

Perhaps our greatest need today is for a more mature understanding of our responsibilities in respect to the electoral process. 'It is necessary that every one should conscientiously take an active part in the election of these Assemblies . . .' Shoghi Effendi states. He further enjoins us 'to consider without the least trace of passion and prejudice, and irrespective of any material consideration, the names of only those who can best combine the necessary qualities of *unquestioned loyalty*, of *selfless devotion*, of a *well-trained mind*, of *recognized ability* and *mature experience*.'[13]*

Some questions we might ask ourselves are: Do we vote for someone simply because we have a personal attachment to them? Do we vote for someone only because he or she appears to have a high social or professional status in the world? Do we vote for someone only because he is a dynamic speaker, or because he inspires or amuses us on the platform? Do we look only at those who are in the limelight, or do we seek for the above qualities as evidenced in less visible services to the Cause of God? All of these and many other conditions may be present in a well-qualified individual, but they are not sufficient or even important in themselves, unless the qualities named by the Guardian are present to the highest degree available, in our prayerful judgment.

Sometimes a Bahá'í, perhaps newly arrived in an area, will feel that he lacks sufficient information and knowledge to permit him to cast his vote wisely. Concerning this, Shoghi Effendi has stated: 'This distinguishing right which the believer possesses . . . does not carry with it nor does it imply an obligation to cast his vote, if he feels that the circumstances under which he lives do not justify or allow him to exercise that right intelligently and with understanding. This is a matter which should be left to the individual to decide himself according to his own conscience and discretion.'[14] Such an individual, however, should attend his state, district, or provincial convention if at all possible in order to advance his eligibility as a voter.

*italics added

Casting a ballot in a Bahá'í election is a very sacred act. Only careful deliberation can prevent us from wasting this spiritual opportunity.

The Gift of God Within each Community

Criticism and backbiting destroy the spirit whether they are directed against individuals or institutions. There is always room for constructive suggestions and recommendations to be made to the Spiritual Assembly, but criticism amongst community members creates a negative atmosphere within the community that affects all. There is only one way to happiness and fulfillment in community life. The Universal House of Justice has shown us the way:

The friends are called upon to give their wholehearted support and cooperation to the Local Spiritual Assembly, first by voting for the membership and then by energetically pursuing its plans and programs, by turning to it in time of trouble or difficulty, by praying for its success and taking delight in its rise to influence and honor. This great prize, this gift of God within each community must be cherished, nurtured, loved, assisted, obeyed and prayed for.[15]

2

The Birth of a World Community

'The Bahá'ís of the World'

The hundredth anniversary year of the martyrdom of the Báb in 1950 marked a new stage in the development of the Bahá'í community. This organism had now grown to such a stature that, in the eyes of Shoghi Effendi, Guardian of the Bahá'í Faith, it could be considered a *world* community. His Riḍván message of that year joyously recounted victories in the 'Eastern and Western hemispheres, gathered from diverse classes, creeds and colors'. From this time forward he addressed many messages to the 'Bahá'ís of the world', through the National Assemblies, calling them for the first time to collective undertakings.

This new emphasis was felt immediately as Shoghi Effendi issued an appeal to the 'entire body of believers' to collaborate in the completion of the superstructure of the Shrine of the Báb, an enterprise which he said transcended that of any national institution. As a river, nearing the sea, widens to receive the swifter flow, so did this year also mark an acceleration in all aspects of the evolution of the Faith. Within the course of three eventful years, this new emphasis led to the launching of the mighty Ten Year World Crusade in 1953 whose goals reached throughout the planet and which drew together the forces of all existing National Assemblies, then but twelve in number. It also inaugurated an administrative evolution that would have the strongest impact on the future of the Cause of God.

A Year of Decision

By the close of 1951 Shoghi Effendi had set in motion the initial stages for the establishment of two mighty arms of the Administrative Order of the Faith. The first of these, the International Bahá'í Council, appointed by him in January of that year, was destined in little more than a decade to evolve into the supreme administrative institution: The Universal House of Justice. Time would witness, cabled Shoghi Effendi, 'its transformation into [a] duly elected body, its efflorescence into [the] Universal House of Justice, and its final fruition through erection of manifold auxiliary institutions constituting the World Administrative Center destined to arise and function and remain permanently established in close neighborhood of Twin Holy Shrines'.[16]

This forerunner of the future House of Justice had its genesis in the Tablet of Carmel revealed by Bahá'u'lláh, which was concerned with the development of the World Center and its institutions. This Tablet was one of the three Divine Charters which Shoghi Effendi wrote had 'set in motion three distinct processes'* operable in the evolution of the Faith.

* See *Messages to the Bahá'í World*, pp. 84-5.

The Bahá'í Council, functioning in the Holy Land, assisted the Guardian in establishing relationships with the newly-emerged State of Israel (created in 1948 through an action of the United Nations General Assembly); in negotiations in matters of personal status with civil authorities; in the erection of the superstructure of the Shrine of the Báb, and later the International Archives building. Under the Guardian's direction, it was instrumental in the acquiring of vitally needed land surrounding the sacred edifices on Mount Carmel and 'Akká, as well as the site for the future Ma_sh_riqu'l-A_dh_kár of the Holy Land.

The appointment of the Bahá'í Council, he further stated, was an event that history would 'acclaim as the greatest event shedding luster upon second epoch of Formative Age . . .' This epoch had begun in 1944, the 100th anniversary of the birth of the Faith, and was marked by the successful conclusion of the First Seven Year Plan given to America by the Guardian in accordance with 'Abdu'l-Bahá's *Tablets of the Divine Plan*, the Divine Charter for teaching the Faith throughout the world.

The other arm of the Administrative Order, the institution of the Hands of the Cause of God, had its impetus in the appointment by Shoghi Effendi of twelve Hands of the Cause of God on December 24, 1951. This was followed a few weeks later by an additional contingent of seven, nineteen in all. In the course of a few more years its membership would reach 'thrice nine', or twenty-seven in all. This institution was to grow and expand until its seal would be set in the formation of the International Teaching Center in the Holy Land under the auspices of the Universal House of Justice in June 1973.

The twofold sacred functions of the Hands of the Cause, in conformity with 'Abdu'l-Bahá's *Will and Testament*, the Divine Charter for the development of the institutions of the Faith, were: 'the propagation and preservation of the unity of the Faith of Bahá'u'lláh.'

In the Tablet of the World Bahá'u'lláh had conferred special blessings upon the members of this institution, asking God 'to shield them through the power of His hosts, to protect them through the potency of His dominion and to aid them through His indomitable strength which prevaileth over all created things'.[17] None could foretell the weighty import of those words — how in six swiftly passing years, that shield, protection and strength invoked by Bahá'u'lláh would be put to full test and meaning to all Bahá'ís of the world, and to the Hands of the Cause of God themselves.

Auxiliary Boards Appointed as Deputies of Hands of the Cause

The Hands of the Cause of God had little time to prepare themselves as 'chosen instruments' for their role in the Guardian's great Crusade. Fifteen Hands, outside the Holy Land, were destined to serve as the 'standard-bearers' in five continents. They would begin by attending the four inter-continental conferences in Africa, America, Europe and Asia associated with the observance of Holy Year* and the launching of the Ten Year Plan. But how could they extend their reach to all the communities within those wide expanses? The answer came

---

* The hundredth anniversary of the first intimation of Bahá'u'lláh's revelation in the Siyáh-Chál.

from Shoghi Effendi. Effective at Riḍván 1954, they were directed to appoint an Auxiliary Board for each continent to serve as their 'deputies, assistants, advisers'. Thirty-six Bahá'ís were named in these first, historic appointments, nine members each in Africa, America and Europe, and nine in Asia and Australasia.

Board members were each assigned a territory, and, under the direction of their respective Hands, set to work for the execution of the Plan. They had no administrative functions, but their work involved periodic visits to Bahá'í centers, groups and assemblies — stimulating, encouraging and increasing their awareness of the spiritual challenge and responsibility now resting upon them. Shoghi Effendi stressed the work of the pioneers in the field, and urged the Board members to keep in touch with them, help them to *persevere*, to remain at their posts at all costs and to be 'aware of the great station of service to which they have been called . . .'

Few hard and fast rules of operation were given by the Guardian — decisions could be made later, he stated, in the light of experience. He was anxious for them to get on with the work of the Crusade; but his Riḍván 1954 message clearly foreshadowed their forthcoming role in the 'sacred task of safeguarding the Faith'.

Reorientation in Respect to Funds

The scope of Bahá'í giving had hitherto been largely focused upon two funds: local and national. The emergence of these destined world-encircling institutions of the Faith required a 'reorientation' in this vital aspect of Bahá'í activity and resulted in the implementation of two new funds. The first of these, the Bahá'í International Fund, grew out of the rise and consolidation of the World Administrative Center in the Holy Land with its responsibility for a speedily evolving world community. Both national and local Spiritual Assemblies, the Guardian wrote, must in future consider this new fund their 'spiritual obligation'. Moreover, he stated, 'participation of individual believers, through contributions directly transmitted to the Holy Land are imperative and beyond the scope of the jurisdiction of National and local assemblies'.[18]

Now the 'lifeblood of the Cause' began also to flow freely to the 'heart of the world', not only from institutions but from individual believers, nourishing the whole body of the Cause and expanding the spiritual bounty of giving.

Three years later, in 1954, five Continental Bahá'í Funds were inaugurated by the Guardian to support the activities of the Hands of the Cause and their soon-to-be-appointed Auxiliary Boards. Shoghi Effendi initiated these funds by contributing five thousand pounds himself, and by the naming of the five Trustees charged with the handling of the funds. He issued a call to assemblies and individuals to contribute regularly to this fund in the future.

'Fervently supplicating at the Holy Threshold', Shoghi Effendi cabled on April 6, 1954, 'for an unprecedented measure of blessings on this vital and indispensable organ of the embryonic and steadily unfolding Bahá'í Administrative Order, presaging the World Order of Bahá'u'lláh . . .'

Each of these new funds — international and continental — were thus established by the Guardian, administered independently by the institutions involved, and directly connected with all the Bahá'ís of the world.

The Working of Three Divine Charters

The two emerging, imminently world-embracing institutions and the great World Crusade itself (a universal expression of the Master's Divine Plan — the Divine Charter for spreading the Faith throughout the world) all had their roots in the Revelation of Bahá'u'lláh and His Covenant, a Covenant uniquely protected by 'Abdu'l-Bahá, Center of the Covenant, and later by Shoghi Effendi, appointed as Guardian of the Faith in the *Will and Testament of 'Abdu'l-Bahá.*

As the goals of the Crusade unfolded and were gradually achieved by the united effort of a rapidly expanding world community, the significance of these newly-founded institutions came into sharp focus. By the triumphant close of the Crusade and the formation of the Universal House of Justice at Riḍván 1963, Bahá'ís throughout the world, now functioning under fifty-six National Spiritual Assemblies, could look down from this high plateau of achievement and see clearly how the workings of the three Divine Charters had been executed in simultaneous orchestration through the inspired vision and direction of their beloved Guardian.

3

The Stewardship of the Hands
of the Cause of God

The Institution of the Hands of the Cause Enters a New Phase

A cablegram of June 4, 1957 from Shoghi Effendi announced that the institution of the Hands of the Cause of God was entering a new phase in the unfoldment of its mission. In addition to assisting the National Assemblies in the effective prosecution of the World Crusade, this body henceforth had a primary obligation 'to watch over and insure protection to the Bahá'í world community, in close collaboration with these same National Assemblies'.

The urgent need for the protective functions to be firmly embedded in the administrative structure of the Faith was stressed by the Guardian, the wisdom of which was to become manifest within a very short time. He reminded the believers of the Master's stern warnings in respect to both internal and external enemies, their persistent machinations to thwart the progress of the Cause of God, to 'misrepresent its purpose, disrupt its administrative institutions, dampen the zeal and sap the loyalty of its supporters'.

The recent victories the Cause had enjoyed — the rise of imposing edifices in the Holy Land and elsewhere in the world; the conferences held in four continents to launch the Crusade which had attracted favorable attention from many world leaders; and the sudden spread of the Faith on a global scale — all of this was serving to awaken fresh animosity and envy among those who had long hoped for the Faith of Bahá'u'lláh to be cast into oblivion. These 'forces of darkness' against which the Army of Light was destined to be arrayed would come not only from 'the unquenchable animosity of its Muslim opponents', but 'new adversaries in the Christian fold', as well as 'old and new Covenant-breakers'.[19]

The Hands of the Cause named Chief Stewards

It was with untold blessings for the future, not even dimly anticipated by those nearest the Guardian, that in October 1957 he brought the total of the Hands of the Cause to its final twenty-seven members. They were, from this moment forth, 'the Chief Stewards of Bahá'u'lláh's embryonic World Commonwealth, who have been invested by the unerring Pen of the Center of His Covenant with the dual function of guarding over the security, and of insuring the propagation, of His Father's Faith'.[20] Commensurate with their new and 'sacred responsibility as protectors of the Faith', the Hands were called upon by Shoghi Effendi to name an additional Auxiliary Board, 'equal in membership to the existing one, and charged with the specific duty of watching over the security of the Faith'. This new Board would complement the functions of the original Board whose services were now exclusively directed toward the prosecution of the Ten Year Plan.

'The Unerring Pen'

It was the 'unerring Pen' of 'Abdu'l-Bahá that had set forth in His Will and Testament, the last of the Divine Charters to be revealed to the Bahá'ís, the manner of appointment and the duties and obligations of the Hands of the Cause. This sacred document, unique in the history of religion, had given the Bahá'ís some foreknowledge of the scope of this institution and the station of its members. Furthermore, the Guardian had bestowed posthumous appointments upon certain distinguished believers, such as Siyyid Muṣṭafá Rúmí, Louis Gregory, Martha Root, Keith Ransom-Kehler, John E. Esslemont, Ḥájí Abu'l-Ḥasan (Ḥájí Amín), John Henry Hyde-Dunn, Roy Wilhelm, 'Abdu'l-Jalíl Bey Sa'd, Muḥammad Taqíy-i-Iṣfahání, and other Bahá'ís of both East and West.

According to the Master's Will, the Hands of the Cause could only be appointed by the Guardian of the Faith. Their obligations, He stated, were 'to diffuse the Divine Fragrances, to edify the souls of men, to promote learning, to improve the character of all men and to be at all times and under all conditions sanctified and detached from earthly things. They must manifest the fear of God by their conduct, their manners, their deeds and their words.'

In the sacred Texts, many passages refer to 'the learned': to 'the learned ones in Bahá' in the *Kitáb-i-Aqdas*; to the 'rulers and the learned among the people of Bahá' in the *Kitáb-i-'Ahd*, the book of Bahá'u'lláh's Covenant; blessings and protection are invoked for them in the Tablet of the World. Among the many references that appear in this respect in *The Secret of Divine Civilization*, 'Abdu'l-Bahá cites the following attributes and duties devolving upon these servants: 'to fear God, to love God by loving His servants, to exercise mildness and forbearance and calm, to be sincere, amenable, clement and compassionate; to have resolution and courage, trustworthiness and energy, to strive and struggle, to be generous, loyal, without malice, to have zeal and a sense of honor, to be high-minded and magnanimous . . .'[21] Shoghi Effendi quotes many references to the learned in *God Passes By.*

Although the believers were familiar with many of these passages, the relationship to the Institution of the Hands of the Cause was not as yet understood generally by the Bahá'ís. Understanding and appreciation of this institution unfolded gradually and steadily as the love, devotion and example of the Hands of the Cause throughout all continents permeated the world community, directly affecting institutions and personal lives alike.

The March of the Institutions

Shoghi Effendi bestowed a last precious gift upon the Bahá'ís of the world: five great gatherings to be held throughout the world in 1958 — days of praise and thanksgiving to Bahá'u'lláh for the victories won since the great Plan had been launched five years before. Now, midway in the Plan, Bahá'í pioneers were scattered throughout all continents and major island groups: from the Arctic Ocean to the Falkland Islands; from Spitzbergen to Madagascar; through much of Asia, and the Islands of the Atlantic and Pacific. *Bahá'í News*, an international news journal, pictured their successes in the form of photographs of Local Spiritual Assemblies, showing the pioneers and their newly-found cohorts gathered like rare pearls from the shores of their adopted homeland. They were a source of wonder and gratitude to those who had not yet ventured into the foreign field.

'Now', said the Hand of the Cause Dhikru'lláh Khádem, 'the Cause has become truly universal through the vision of Shoghi Effendi!'

Each conference received the Guardian's representative who at that time served both as a Hand of the Cause and as a member of the International Bahá'í Council. The presence of Hands of the Cause of both East and West at all conferences, along with their succeeding travels to many lands, brought large numbers of believers into close association with them, enhancing the meaning and value of this institution.

'These joyous convocations', the beloved Guardian wrote, were 'dedicated to the glorification of His Name, and expressly convened for the purpose of accelerating the march of the institutions of His world-redeeming Order, and of hastening the establishment of His Kingdom in the hearts of men.'[22]

In these few words are contained the essence of the broad goals toward which Bahá'ís have directed their efforts and their dreams since the utterances of Bahá'u'lláh first set in motion His grand redemptive plan for the salvation of mankind. *They marked the Guardian's final earthly call to the Bahá'ís of the world.*

The Root of Belief

Whatever the Forces at work behind the visible scenes, not fully understood by finite minds, the results were pure miracle. Looking back a few years later, with profound gratitude, the Bahá'ís could clearly see the hand of divine guidance working at a superhuman pace through its chosen instrument, their Guardian. In less than seven years he had galvanized the entire world community of believers into Bahá'u'lláh's Army of Light and given it the spiritual World Crusade as an arena for this unified action. He had hastened the growth of its twelve National Spiritual Assemblies in varying degrees and made them the 'generals' of this planetary operation. He had brought into existence the institution of the Hands of the Cause of God and designated its members as the 'standard-bearers' of the Crusade as well as the 'Chief Stewards' of the Faith. And he had instituted the International Bahá'í Council as the first stage in the evolvement of the Universal House of Justice, the supreme administrative body of the Faith: *'source of all good and freed from all error.'*

As the believers gathered in their conferences in 1958, consoled by their 'standard-bearers' in the loss of their beloved Commander, the station of 'Chief Stewards', so recently bestowed upon the Hands of the Cause, shone forth like a beacon. With one heart and mind the Bahá'ís arose to give them complete allegiance and vowed to bring total victory to the Guardian's World Crusade. The defection of one Hand of the Cause two years later (Charles Mason Remey), through a claim to be the 'hereditary Guardian', created only a tiny ripple on the sea of Bahá'í certitude and was destined to fragment itself in foam upon the rock of Bahá'u'lláh's Covenant.*

What the Bahá'ís felt and experienced during those poignant months is expressed most vividly in the words of

* The meaning of Covenant-breaking is explored in the next chapter.

Amatu'l-Bahá Rúḥíyyih Khánum, Hand of the Cause of God and Shoghi Effendi's devoted wife and companion of twenty years: 'Perhaps at no point in its history will the deepness of the root of belief that binds the Bahá'ís to their religion be again laid as bare as it was in the year after the passing of Shoghi Effendi. They bowed their heads in the agony of the grief that swept them, but they held.'[23]

Their Shining Hour

Shortly after the passing of Shoghi Effendi, the Hands of the Cause gathered in the Holy Land 'determined to carry out every aspect of the Guardian's expressed wishes and hopes'. Aware of the dangers that existed to the unity of the Faith they wrote to the believers: 'By consecration of spirit we are armed against all manner of assault, and we hold the weapon of faith with which the triumph of the Guardian's aims and purpose is assured.'[24]

To read this first Proclamation of the Hands of the Cause more than a quarter of a century after it was written is to marvel at its courage and vision. It was written only a few weeks after the passing of Shoghi Effendi by his 'standard-bearers', whose hearts and minds held a cup of grief unimagined only a short time before. Plans were made for the formation of the Universal House of Justice — the preliminary steps having been outlined by the Guardian. Nine Hands were selected, as ordained in 'Abdu'l-Bahá's *Will and Testament,* to remain at the World Center as a nucleus to conduct the day-to-day affairs of the Faith. A yearly convocation of all Hands of the Cause was scheduled. Those not serving at the World Center traveled throughout the world, giving of themselves unceasingly to the believers, encouraging them to win every goal of the Guardian's great Plan. At Riḍván 1961 the Hands supervised the election of the International Bahá'í Council, one of the evolutionary stages in establishing the House of Justice. This first Bahá'í election of an international scope was conducted by postal ballot by the members of the thirty-one existing National Spiritual Assemblies.

London, now sheltering the precious remains of Shoghi Effendi, was selected as the site for the Most Great Jubilee at Riḍván 1963, a great World Congress called for by the Guardian in the World Crusade goals.

Bahá'ís throughout the world were thrilled by the leadership of their Chief Stewards, their hopes uplifted, and their responses galvanized into action. Victory after victory poured in. Each year more National Assemblies were formed. Bahá'í Temples in Africa, Australia and Germany were dedicated or brought near to completion.

For six years the revered Hands of the Cause, acting as the Chief Stewards of the Faith as called upon by Shoghi Effendi, diligently carried out the directives contained in his messages, going not a hair's breadth beyond his clear guidance. Their final act was to convene the International Convention in the Holy Land that elected the first, historic Universal House of Justice at Riḍván 1963. Then, with grace, humility and love, the twenty-two remaining Hands laid down the scepter of their brief and illustrious leadership as Chief Stewards before that Supreme Body. *It was their shining hour.* Surely religious history offers no parallel to these 'faithful and wise steward[s] whom [the] master . . . set over his household', to cite a befitting parable of Jesus.

4

The Meaning of Covenant-breaking

The Center of the Covenant

'What is the greatest characteristic of the Revelation of Bahá'u'lláh?' The question was being asked by a teacher at a summer school class. There was silence. There are many conditions, qualities, laws and requisites that are in varying stations of preeminence in the Revelation.

'Abdu'l-Bahá had Himself answered the question just three days before boarding the ship that would take Him from the shores of America. It was December 3, 1912, in the Kinney home in New York City: 'The most great characteristic of the Revelation of Bahá'u'lláh — a specific teaching not given by any of the prophets of the past,' He said, 'is the ordination and appointment of the Center of the Covenant.'25

He wanted to write it indelibly upon the hearts and minds of His listeners gathered on that late autumn day. The future of His Father's Faith depended upon it. Without full understanding and acceptance of the implications of this appointment by Bahá'u'lláh, the little community of Bahá'ís, already buffeted by storms raised by one who had once been its most dynamic teacher in America,* would be wind-tossed and helpless, its unity eventually shattered and lost.

The Master continued His explanation: 'By this appointment and provision He has safeguarded and protected the religion of God against differences and schisms, making it impossible for anyone to create a new sect or faction of belief . . . The Book of the Covenant or Testament of Bahá'u'lláh is the means of preventing such a possibility, for whosoever shall speak from the authority of himself alone shall be degraded.'[26]

The appointment of 'Abdu'l-Bahá as the Center of the Covenant, the Interpreter and Exemplar of the Faith of Bahá'u'lláh, has its roots in the *Kitáb-i-'Ahd*, the Book of Bahá'u'lláh's Covenant, written entirely by His own hand. It is mentioned succinctly in the *Kitáb-i-Aqdas* and in the Tablet of the Branch. It is sometimes known as the Lesser Covenant (the Greater Covenant having been fulfilled by the coming of the Manifestation, Bahá'u'lláh), and names both the Center of the Covenant and the House of Justice as future centers of infallible guidance and authority.

'When the ocean of My presence hath ebbed and the Book of My Revelation is ended, turn your faces toward Him Whom God hath purposed, Who hath branched from this Ancient Root. The object of this sacred Verse is none other except the Most mighty Branch.'[27]

The story of the tribulation that surrounded 'Abdu'l-

---

* Dr. Khayru'lláh of Chicago, Illinois, once a most active teacher of the Faith in America, who became blinded by ambition to share 'Abdu'l-Bahá's authority, and became a Covenant-breaker. See Shoghi Effendi, *God Passes By*, and H. M. Balyuzi, *'Abdu'l-Bahá*.

Bahá throughout His lifetime, as He labored to uphold the Station conferred upon Him by Bahá'u'lláh, is told elsewhere. His compassion and loving kindness to friend and foe was known to all — but He was leonine in His defense of the Covenant and His protection of the believers against Covenant-breakers.

The Substance of Covenant-breaking

What is Covenant-breaking? Throughout religious history there have been those who out of lust for power, through egotism or jealousy have, after accepting the Light of a new Revelation, risen against it, either to extinguish the Light or to seize authority for themselves.

'The case of all of them resembleth the violation of the Covenant by Judas Iscariot and his followers', 'Abdu'l-Bahá wrote in a letter to the Spiritual Assembly of Los Angeles.[28]

Disobedience to the supreme authority in the Faith, efforts to discredit their position, or to lead off a faction according to one's own interpretation — these form the substance from which Covenant-breaking takes root. This ultimate form of rebellion has occurred at each turning point or transitional stage in the Faith when the scepter of authority passed from one Center to another: from Bahá'u'lláh to 'Abdu'l-Bahá, from 'Abdu'l-Bahá to Shoghi Effendi; and again under the stewardship of the Hands of the Cause of God leading to the establishment of the Universal House of Justice.*

* The defection of a Hand of the Cause in 1960, who had previously signed the Proclamation of the Hands and succeeding documents for nearly three years, brought the reality of Covenant-breaking into sharp relief for the many new believers who had not lived through any such experience before.

Often the initial thrust has come from a family member
or relative too close to the Light to see its full brilliance.
Amatu'l-Bahá Ruḥíyyih Khánum writes an illuminating
chapter on this in her book *The Priceless Pearl*, entitled
'The Principle of Light and Shadow':

The principle of light and shadow, setting each other off, the
one intensifying the other, is seen in nature and in history . . .
the brighter the light the darker the shadow; the evil in men
calls to mind the good, and the greatness of the good under-
lines the evil. The entire life of the Guardian was plagued and
blighted by the ambition, the folly, the jealousy and hatred of
individuals who rose up against the Cause and against him as
Head of the Cause and who thought they could either subvert
the Faith entirely or discredit its Guardian and set themselves
up as leaders of a rival faction and win the body of believers
over to their own interpretation of the Teachings and the way
in which they believed the Cause of God should be run. No one
ever succeeded in doing these things, but a series of disaffected
individuals never ceased to try.[29]

Are Covenant-breakers aware of what they do? In a letter of
July 24, 1919 to Mrs Corinne True, early American
Bahá'í, later named a Hand of the Cause by Shoghi
Effendi, the Master wrote: 'These do not doubt the
validity of the Covenant, but selfish motives have dragged
them to this condition.'[30]

And again to Martha Root during the same month:
'This is because of their personal motives, for they had
thought of securing leadership and wealth, but when they
considered that in remaining firm in the Covenant their
purpose would not be realized they deviated from it.'[31]

Covenant-breaking can take an open form, or be secret
and furtive. It was the latter method about which the
Master and the Guardian so strongly warned the

believers. 'Abdu'l-Bahá said, using an old but sharply effective analogy: 'They appear as sheep, and in reality are ferocious wolves.'

History demonstrates that Covenant-breakers try to appear as devoted believers, 'in pious garb', quoting the sacred Writings effusively but distorting them to serve their own ulterior purpose. 'Probably no group of people in the world have softer tongues, or proclaim more loudly their innocence, than those who in their heart of hearts, and by every act, are enemies of the Center of the Covenant,' Shoghi Effendi wrote. 'The Master well knew this and that is why He said we must shun their company, but pray for them.'[32]

Pray for them? On the cross, Jesus prayed for those including Judas Iscariot, who through abject cruelty or lack of spiritual consciousness had precipitated His death: 'Father, forgive them for they know not what they do.'

Those who labored throughout their lives to destroy the Master, and later to bring down the Guardian, knew well what they were doing; yet the Master could pray: 'O my Lord, Have mercy upon them . . . grant that all trials and hardships may be the lot of this servant . . .'[33]

The First Principle to Grasp

To shun completely the company of Covenant-breakers is the first and most essential principle for a believer to grasp. Here is the Guardian's warning:

'Bahá'u'lláh and the Master in many places and very emphatically have told us to shun entirely all Covenant-breakers as they are afflicted with what we might try and define as a contagious spiritual disease . . . These souls are not lost forever

. . . God will forgive any soul if he repents. Most of them don't
want to repent, unfortunately . . .'[34]

One would not knowingly expose himself to cholera or
plague, or walk into a pit of vipers and expect no harm to
himself. 'Abdu'l-Bahá, the essence of love and forbearance, nevertheless states forcefully in His *Will and
Testament:* '. . . the beloved of God must entirely shun
them, avoid them, foil their machinations and evil whis-
perings, guard the Law of God and His religion . . .'
When He speaks of foiling their machinations He does
not mean the individual Bahá'í to enter into controversy
with Covenant-breakers or to try and persuade them of
the error of their ways. The above warnings predicate the
exact opposite of such action. The institutions of the Faith
alone are designed and equipped, through the power of
the Covenant of Bahá'u'lláh, to investigate any situation
that arises in this respect and to take protective care.
Although all institutions are protectors of the Faith, the
institution of the learned that had its inception with the
appointment of the Hands of the Cause is especially
committed to 'watch over and insure protection to the
Bahá'í world community'. Deepening the believers in an
understanding of the Covenant is the fundamental obligation of the Auxiliary Board for Protection.
'Abdu'l-Bahá's admonition to the Hands of the Cause to
'be ever watchful' now devolves especially upon the
Boards of Counselors.

In likening Covenant-breaking to the most virulent
disease, He made clear that it was a spiritual disease, that
it was highly contagious and could quickly affect others
who, out of curiosity, naïveté, or wrongly held notions of

'independent investigation' might subject themselves to this grave risk. More than any other spiritual affliction, Covenant-breaking carries the power to destroy the soul. And even as a cancer must be removed from the body of a patient lest it spread and bring death to other parts, so must the cancer of violation of the Covenant of God be removed from the body of the community of true believers.

'For so grievous is the conduct and behavior of this false people', warns the Master in His *Will and Testament,* 'that they are become even as an axe striking at the very root of the Blessed Tree. Should they be suffered to continue they would . . . exterminate the Cause of God, His Word, and themselves.'

Herein lies both warning and assurance. For over six thousand years God has guided His people forward along the path of history leading to the 'broad uplands of the Most Great Peace'. In spite of divisiveness within and between religions of the world, in spite of shattered hopes, faith in the coming of the Kingdom of God on earth and in the brotherhood of man has never been completely extinguished in the hearts of the lovers of God. For Bahá'u'lláh has not only fulfilled the Covenant of God, He has traced its golden thread from Adam, through all the Prophets of the past, to this Great Day. He has tied it securely to institutions He Himself ordained so that no destroyer can, however hard he may persevere, 'exterminate the Cause of God'.

The Second Principle

The second principle a believer needs to observe in

respect to Covenant-breaking relates to his own actions should he think he has observed signs of this aberration in others. The individual believer need have no fear. If he has such concern he should *not* first attempt to prove or disprove his fears. He should immediately contact an institution of the Faith — a Hand of the Cause, a Counselor, an Auxiliary Board member or assistant, a Spiritual Assembly, national or local — whichever it is most practical to contact, or to which he feels moved to turn. Because of the Counselors' special protective functions it is important that they be advised quickly — therefore, notifying one's Auxiliary Board member for protection, regardless of what other institutions are advised, is vital. The Board of Counselors and the National Assembly involved are always in complete cooperation in handling matters of protection, but it is the Counselors who make direct investigation of the matter, usually assigning an Auxiliary Board member for protection to the initial task.

No individual should designate someone as a Covenant-breaker unless and until the process of investigation by the institutions involved has been carried out. Every care and caution is taken to help the individual who appears to be affected by this aberration to correct his understanding and behavior. Only after the most careful, prayerful, detailed and thorough investigation has been made does the Board of Counselors convey its findings to the International Teaching Center in the Holy Land and a decision is made by that body. Yet one more step is required: this decision must be ratified by the Universal House of Justice. At this point the community is advised and then disassociation with the Covenant-breaker takes effect, although the institutions may find it advisable to give some cautionary advice prior to this. A believer should not be naïve. He should be alert to any sign of Covenant-breaking, knowing he has access to the protection of the institutions that he serves and that in turn serve him. 'Empower us then, O my God, to spread abroad Thy signs among Thy creatures, and to guard Thy Faith in Thy realm,' is a prayer for each Bahá'í.

What Covenant-breaking Is Not

What about someone who has withdrawn his membership in the Faith, or who states he no longer believes in Bahá'u'lláh? What about the believer who has had sanctions placed upon him, or who has lost his administrative rights? Are they to be avoided by Bahá'ís? These situations have no connection with Covenant-breaking. They are under the authority of the National Spiritual Assembly. While efforts are made by all concerned to assist a Bahá'í whose faith is weak and faltering, no one is prevented from leaving the Bahá'í community, and the degree and amount of association with former members of the Faith is up to the individuals concerned. As in all things involving the Cause of God, it becomes a question of how the Faith itself is best served.

In respect to administrative sanctions applied to a Bahá'í who has knowingly violated Bahá'u'lláh's laws or has repeatedly been a disruptive force in the community, this action is not punitive in intent or application but rather curative in purpose. The individual involved is still a Bahá'í if he believes in Bahá'u'lláh, although much of his association in community affairs is restricted or curtailed. He is, for the time, suspended at that point where the threads of justice and mercy are woven together. Through his own sincere efforts and prayers, through a change in behavior, and through the prayers and assistance of other believers he can be restored again to full communion with his fellow-believers, leaving behind his former difficulties. Again, the understanding of Bahá'ís in many such cases has helped restore such believers to their full status in the Faith where they have become faithful and productive members.

Enemies of the Cause of God

Although it is strongly recommended to Bahá'ís by the Master, the Guardian and now by the Universal House of Justice that Bahá'ís 'avoid and ignore material prepared and circulated by the Covenant-breakers', they also state that 'books by well-meaning yet unenlightened enemies of the Cause can be read so as to refute their charges'. There are exceptions to this in respect to certain individuals who are neither well-meaning nor unenlightened and who expend great effort in viciously attacking and distorting the true meaning of the Faith. In the cases of such avowed enemies of the Cause, the protective agencies of the Faith often advise strict avoidance by the believers, both of the persons involved as well as their writings.

The Covenant of God, renewed by the coming of the Báb and Bahá'u'lláh, upheld and protected by 'Abdu'l-Bahá, Shoghi Effendi and now the Universal House of Justice, is a 'spiritual contract'. Our loyalty to this contract, in the words of the Master, makes us a 'party of the Covenant'.

'Today the dynamic power of the world of existence is the power of the Covenant which like unto an artery pulsateth in the body of the contingent world and protecteth Bahá'í unity.'[35]

It is that power that inspired the Bahá'ís, though few in number, to undertake at the Master's bidding the formidable task of raising the Mother Temple of the world in Wilmette, Illinois. It stirred them into launching the great Teaching Plans initiated by Shoghi Effendi, culminating in the world-encircling Ten Year World Crusade that drew upon the resources of all national communities. It moved the believers throughout the globe to rally around their Chief Stewards, and spurred them into achieving a ringing victory in the World Crusade; and to inaugurate the first, historic Universal House of Justice now occupying its magnificent seat on the Mountain of God.

5

The Unassailable Foundation

A New Epoch Unfolds in the Formative Age

'It was in obedience to the summons of the Lord of Hosts Himself', wrote the Universal House of Justice, 'that the elected representatives of the fifty-six national and regional communities of the Bahá'í world were called to elect, in the shadow of God's Holy Mountain and in the house of the Center of His Covenant, the members of the Universal House of Justice.'[36]

A new epoch in the Formative Age had opened to the Bahá'í world!

This historic election conjoined with other events of deep significance. It marked the hundredth anniversary of the Declaration of Bahá'u'lláh in Baghdád, and the fulfillment of the prophecy in Daniel, cited by 'Abdu'l-Bahá, concerning the 'thousand three hundred and thirty-five days'. The formation of this Supreme Body in the Holy Land was followed immediately by the celebration of the Most Great Jubilee in London 'permeated by a spirit of such bliss as could only have come from the outpourings of the Abhá Kingdom'. The Jubilee drew more than 6,000

Bahá'ís from all continents and distant islands of the sea, from every kind and color of the family of man. Streams of believers came daily in loving remembrance to the Guardian's resting-place in this great western city. Joy and thanksgiving filled the air as victories of the Guardian's great Crusade, now ended, were recounted.

Six months following the Jubilee the House of Justice announced:

After prayerful and careful study of the Holy Texts bearing upon the question of the appointment of the successor to Shoghi Effendi as Guardian of the Cause of God, and after prolonged consultation which included consideration of the views of the Hands of the Cause of God residing in the Holy Land, the Universal House of Justice finds that there is no way to appoint or to legislate to make it possible to appoint a second Guardian to succeed Shoghi Effendi.

Only the Supreme Body, the Universal House of Justice, had the authority with which to make this pronouncement. In a later lengthy message they shared an explanation of the powers and prerogatives of this Supreme Institution ordained by Bahá'u'lláh. 'It should be understood by the friends', they wrote, 'that before legislating upon any matter the Universal House of Justice studies carefully and exhaustively both the Sacred Texts and the writings of Shoghi Effendi on the subject. The interpretations written by the beloved Guardian cover a vast range of subjects and are equally as binding as the Text itself.

The Guardian reveals what the Scripture means, his interpretation is a statement of truth which cannot be varied. Upon the Universal House of Justice, in the words of the Guardian, 'has been conferred the exclusive right of legislating on matters not expressly revealed in the Bahá'í Writings . . .' Although not invested with the function of interpretation, the House of Justice is in a position to do everything necessary to establish the World Order of Bahá'u'lláh on this earth.[37]

'Abdu'l-Bahá had elucidated the subject at length:

'Those matters of major importance which constitute the foundation of the Law of God are explicitly recorded in the Text, but subsidiary laws are left to the House of Justice. The wisdom of this is that the times never remain the same, for change is a necessary quality and an essential attribute of this world, and of time and place.

'Let it not be imagined', He exclaimed, 'that the House of Justice will take any decision according to its own concepts and opinions. God forbid! The Supreme House of Justice will take decisions and establish laws through the inspiration and confirmation of the Holy Spirit, because it is in the safekeeping and under the shelter and protection of the Ancient Beauty, and obedience to its decisions is a bounden and essential duty and an absolute obligation . . .'[38]

Two centers of authority exist in the Faith as a shield and shelter for the Bahá'í community, and to which every believer must turn: one is the Book with its Interpreter — for 'in reality the Interpreter ['Abdu'l-Bahá and Shoghi Effendi] . . . is an extension of that center which is the Word itself'; the other center is the Universal House of Justice 'guided by God to decide on whatever is not explicitly revealed in the Book'.[39]

The Indestructible Covenant

Some years after its original formation, the Universal House of Justice commented on the relationship of the Guardianship to the Universal House of Justice and the dangerous waters safely traversed by the world community of Bahá'ís after the passing of Shoghi Effendi.

'Future Guardians', they wrote, 'are clearly envisaged and referred to in the Writings, but there is nowhere any promise or guarantee that the line of Guardians would endure forever; on the contrary there are clear indications that the line could be broken. Yet in spite of this, there is a repeated insistence in the Writings on the indestructibility of the Covenant and the immutability of God's Purpose for this Day.

One of the most striking passages which envisage the possibility of such a break in the line of Guardians is in the Kitáb-i-Aqdas itself: 'The endowments dedicated to charity revert to God, the Revealer of Signs. No one has the right to lay hold on them without leave from the Dawning-place of Revelation. After Him the decision rests with the Aghsán (Branches), and after them with the House of Justice — should it be established in the world by then — so that they may use these endowments for the benefit of the Sites exalted in this Cause, and for that which they have been commanded by God, the Almighty, the All-Powerful. Otherwise the endowments should be referred to the people of Bahá, who speak not without His leave and who pass no judgment but in accordance with that which God has ordained in this Tablet, they who are the champions of victory betwixt heaven and earth, so that they may spend them on that which has been decreed in the Holy Book by God, the Mighty, the Bountiful.'

The passing of Shoghi Effendi in 1957 precipitated the very situation provided for in this passage, in that the line of Aghsán ended before the House of Justice had been elected. Although, as is seen, the ending of the line of Aghsán at some stage was provided for, we must never underestimate the grievous loss that the Faith has suffered. God's purpose for mankind remains unchanged, however, and the mighty Covenant of Bahá'u'lláh remains impregnable.[40]

It is to the abiding glory of the believers, profoundly vindicatory as is this passage revealed by Bahá'u'lláh, prophetic in its purport, that they had clung to the Covenant, had followed their Chief Stewards steadfastly, and safely bridged the six years between the passing of their Guardian and the formation of the Universal House of Justice. There is a symbolical arch or bridge in religious tradition — 'finer than a hair and sharper than the edge of a sword' — over which the soul must pass after it is weighed, in order to enter Paradise. The entire community of Bahá'ís, barring a few who chose to 'tread the wilderness', safely traversed their 'bridge of al-Ṣiráṭ' and entered the sheltering stronghold of their Universal House of Justice. The Covenant of God, symbolized by the arch of the rainbow in the Old Testament, had delivered them.*

A New Epoch in the Divine Plan

A two-year teaching campaign began in early 1951. For the first time five National Spiritual Assemblies, spearheaded by the British community and including Egypt, India, Iran and the United States cooperated in opening the heart of Africa to the Bahá'í Faith. Just as the African campaign got under way, the formation of the International Bahá'í Council took place. The coinciding of these events had, in the Guardian's words, a 'peculiar

---

* The Báb refers to the Bridge 'sharper than a sword and finer than a hair' that must be traversed on the Day of Resurrection, and also by the soul at the hour of death. See *Selections from the Writings of the Báb*, pp. 44, 96. The Bridge of Chinvat (sometimes Sinvat) is a term used in Parsi or Zoroastrian legends. In Islám it is known by the Arabic term *al-Ṣiráṭ*. This symbolism played a strong part in medieval Christianity, in Buddhist, Hindu and Jewish tradition, and in many tribal myths. See Scribner's *Encyclopedia of Religion and Ethics, Volume II*, and Thomas Y. Crowell Company's *Asiatic Mythology*, 1963, edited by J. Hackin.

significance in the evolution of our beloved Faith ...
heralding the establishment of the Supreme Legislative
Body ...'[41] At that time Shoghi Effendi not only pointed
to a coming world enterprise to be undertaken by all
National Assemblies throughout the Bahá'í World,* but
to similar undertakings that would be launched in a
future epoch by the Universal House of Justice. No one
could foresee that future epoch would begin in little more
than a dozen years when the newly elected House of
Justice launched the Nine Year Plan in 1964!

* This materialized as the Ten Year World Crusade launched in 1953.

6

The Formation of Continental Boards of Counselors

The Extension of Functions of Hands of the Cause into the Future

Thirty years of Shoghi Effendi's ministry had transpired before the foundation of the institution known generically in Bahá'í Scripture as 'the learned' came into active functioning through the appointment by Shoghi Effendi of the nineteen Hands of the Cause of God in 1951–2, followed by the naming of the first Auxiliary Boards at Riḍván 1954. Another twenty years were to elapse before this institution reached its crowning stage in the formation of the International Teaching Center established by the Universal House of Justice in 1973. Accordingly, a half-century of the Formative Age of the Faith flowed down the stream of Bahá'í history before the seal of this institution took its place as the right arm of the Supreme Administrative Body in the Holy Land.

Among three major tasks of the new Nine Year Plan set for the World Center were: (1) Publication of a synopsis and codification of the *Kitáb-i-Aqdas*, the Most Holy Book;

(2) Formulation of the constitution of the Universal House of Justice; (3) Development of the institution of the Hands of the Cause of God . . . with a view to the extension into the future of its appointed functions of protection and propagation.

In respect to the latter task, the Universal House of Justice announced in November of 1964 the following conclusions:

There is no way to appoint, or to legislate to make it possible to appoint, Hands of the Cause of God.

Responsibility for decisions of matters of general policy affecting the institution of the Hands of the Cause, which was formerly exercised by the beloved Guardian, now devolves upon the Universal House of Justice as the supreme and central institution of the Faith to which all must turn.[42]

The work of the Hands of the Cause in respect to protection and propagation in all continents continued apace, with a large increase of Auxiliary Board members — from seventy-two to one hundred and thirty-five.

The House of Justice further stated:

The exalted rank and specific functions of the Hands of the Cause of God make it inappropriate for them to be elected or appointed to administrative institutions, or to be elected as delegates to national conventions. Furthermore it is their desire and the desire of the House of Justice that they be free to devote their entire energies to the vitally important duties conferred upon them in the Holy Writings. The importance of close collaboration between the Hands of the Cause and national spiritual assemblies cannot be overstressed . . .[43]

Thus the work of the Hands of the Cause was greatly supplemented at this time, but the course of its 'extension into the future' was still to come.

An Institution is Born

After four years of 'thought and study' and 'prolonged and prayerful consultation between the Universal House of Justice and the Hands of the Cause of God', the Supreme Body announced its decision: to establish eleven Continental Boards of Counselors for the protection and propagation of the Faith, three boards in Africa, three in the Americas and in Asia, and one each for Australasia and Europe. One member of each Board was named as trustee for the Continental Fund.

'Their duties', the House of Justice stated, 'will include directing the Auxiliary Boards in their respective areas, consulting and collaborating with National Spiritual Assemblies, and keeping the Hands of the Cause and the Universal House of Justice informed concerning the conditions of the Cause in their areas.' The Hands of the Cause in the Holy Land were the liaison between the House of Justice and the Continental Boards of Counselors.

The Hands of the Cause, 'one of the most precious assets the Bahá'í world possesses', were now free to operate on an intercontinental level, pursuing their prime concern for the 'spiritual health of the Bahá'í communities'; to undertake special missions on behalf of the Universal House of Justice; and to assist in the eventual formation of an international teaching center in the Holy Land 'as anticipated in the Guardian's writings'. The formation of new National Assemblies, the gathering of Bahá'ís at oceanic and intercontinental conferences — events of international import — each had a Hand of the Cause of God representing the Supreme Body. The privilege and obligation of the Hands to consult with the

Counselors and with National Spiritual Assemblies on any matter they deemed to be of interest and importance in the Cause was at their own discretion.[44]

'The Counselors and the National Spiritual Assembly have one common objective,' the House of Justice wrote, 'which is service to the Cause and the promotion and protection of its interests. The closer the collaboration between these two institutions the richer will be the divine blessings showered upon them and the community.'

As later stated in the Constitution of the Universal House of Justice, 'a Counselor functions as such only within his zone and should he move his residence out of the zone for which he is appointed he automatically relinquishes his appointment'.

Likewise in that document: 'The rank and specific duties of a Counselor render him ineligible for service on local or national administrative bodies. If elected to the Universal House of Justice he ceases to be a Counselor.'*

'This aloofness, i.e. not serving on assemblies, in itself', the Supreme Body stated earlier, 'provides them with the opportunity to concentrate on the general and vital issues of the Cause, and enables them to provide guidance to the National Spiritual Assemblies, which are usually weighed down with numberless tasks and issues of the day to day work of the community.'

Developing the Art of Collaboration

There was much to be learned, experienced, and put into action as the institutions functioning under Bahá'u'lláh's

---

* The Constitution of the Universal House of Justice was formulated in 1972. The above statement makes it clear that Counselors are eligible for election to the Universal House of Justice under the same conditions as other believers, a sometimes misunderstood point.

terms as 'rulers' and 'learned' developed the method and the atmosphere for their interaction under the guidance of the House of Justice.

'As the Bahá'í world experiences the manifold inter-actions of these two vital and complementary arms of the Administrative Order of Bahá'u'lláh,' the Supreme Body wrote, 'the unique benefits of this divinely ordained System become ever more apparent. The harmonious interaction and the proper discharge of the duties of these institutions representing the rulers and the learned among the people of Bahá is the essential basis at this time for the protection of the Cause of Bahá'u'lláh and the fulfillment of its God-given mandate.'[45]

In respect to the collaboration between Counselors and the National Spiritual Assemblies, Counselor Edna True stated at the North Atlantic Conference in 1971: 'They are severally component parts of the same living organism, and not separate institutions each with its own exclusive, clearly defined responsibilities . . . while certain responsi-bilities have been assigned to each of these institutions, others are shared in common, even though these may be more in the *special* province of one or the other.'

Lines of Authority and Interaction

Especially pertinent to successful interaction was the matter of communication between the two administrative arms and the sharing of information. 'Your most effective collaboration', wrote the House of Justice to the National Assemblies, 'depends largely upon the thoroughness of your mutual exchange of information.' This included an exchange of reports of national committees and Auxiliary

Board members contributing vital information toward the success of the current Plan as well as the protection of the Faith.

Auxiliary Board members were encouraged to make recommendations, along with regular reports, to the Counselors, based upon their observation and experience with the local communities. This enabled the Counselors to draw upon this direct source in offering advice and counsel to National Assemblies, as well as in keeping the World Center fully aware of conditions throughout the world community.

'Authority and direction flow from the Assemblies,' the Supreme Body wrote on October 1, 1969, concerning lines of authority and interaction, 'whereas the power to accomplish the tasks resides primarily in the entire body of the believers.' Stimulating the release of this power was a prime task of the Auxiliary Boards. 'This is a vital activity, and if they are to be able to perform it adequately they must avoid becoming involved in the work of administration.'

It was within the province of the Counselors to deputize an Auxiliary Board member to meet with a National Assembly on occasion, or with a national committee (the assembly concurring), but it should not become regular practice. 'It would diffuse the energies and time of the Auxiliary Board members . . . could lead to the Auxiliary Board member's gradually taking over the direction of the national committee . . . or to his becoming merely a traveling teacher sent hither and thither at the direction of the committee or National Assembly.'

The advantage of Auxiliary Board members making their recommendations through the Counselors rather than directly to National Assemblies or committees can readily be seen. The Counselors, with the broader range and flow of information coming to them, are in a position to better judge the merit of any suggestion or recommendation and thus bring their own knowledge and experience to bear upon it. Also, a short-circuiting of the proper channels of communication would 'undermine the authority of both the Counselors and the National Assembly', the House of Justice warned.[46]

Administrative Counseling

Although Counselors and Board members do not administer or serve on administrative bodies, it does not mean 'that they may not give advice on administrative matters'. It is their responsibility to assist an assembly to function correctly, to make it aware of the Writings that apply to any given situation; or for a Board member to advise the Counselors of any breakdown in the teaching field due to the inefficiency of a national committee. 'Similarly,' the Supreme Body instructed, 'if the Counselors find that a National Spiritual Assembly is not functioning properly, they should not hesitate to consult with the National Spiritual Assembly about this in a frank and loving way.'[47] Moreover, it was left to the discretion of the Counselors as to the manner of their collaboration and consultation with National Assemblies within their zone of operation. 'Unlike other institutions of the Administrative Order, which must function as corporate bodies and decide by majority rule, each Counselor can operate primarily as an individual in the area of responsibility assigned to him by the Board of Counselors.'

Assemblies Set Goals and Plans

Through the workings of the institution of the Counselors, it became a matter of prime concern at all levels of the institution to create support and enthusiasm for the plans and goals of the assemblies. 'The National Spiritual Assembly has the responsibility to formulate its plans and prosecute them. The Boards of Counselors outrank the National institutions of the Faith and are not engaged in the conduct of the administering of these plans', the Supreme Body advised. In performing their tasks of protection and propagation of the Faith, the Board of Counselors 'neither directs nor instructs the Spiritual Assemblies or individual believers, but it has the necessary rank to enable it to ensure that it is kept properly informed and that the Spiritual Assemblies give due consideration to its advice and recommendations. However, the essence of the relationships between Bahá'í institutions is loving consultation and a common desire to serve the Cause of God rather than a matter of rank or station.'[48]

Distinctive Features of the Two Institutions

The Universal House of Justice sent many messages of guidance and inspiration to the Counselors, to National Spiritual Assemblies, and to individuals, illuminating the new pathway of collaboration that had opened throughout the Bahá'í world community. In one of these the Supreme Body quoted Shoghi Effendi in a letter of November 4, 1931, as follows:

In this holy cycle the 'learned' are, on the one hand, the Hands of the Cause of God, and, on the other, the teachers and diffusers of His teachings who do not rank as Hands, but who have attained an eminent position in the teaching work. As to the 'rulers' they refer to members of the Local, National and International Houses of Justice. The duties of each of these souls will be determined in the future.

'The Hands of the Cause of God, the Counselors and the members of the Auxiliary Boards fall within the definition of the "learned" given by the beloved Guardian', the House of Justice wrote, in reference to the above. 'Thus they are all intimately interrelated and it is not incorrect to refer to the three ranks collectively as one institution.' Yet each of these is also an institution in itself. And while the institutions functioning under the terms of 'rulers' and 'learned' were brought into being through the respective processes of election, from the grass roots extendng upward, and by appointment from the Universal House of Justice extending downward, 'a more striking distinction is that whereas the "rulers" in the Cause function as corporate bodies, the "learned" operate primarily as individuals.'[49]

The Role of Love and the Institutions

In a talk given at an annual conference of Hands of the Cause, Counselors and Auxiliary Board members in North America, Dr Jalil Mahmoudi, Auxiliary Board member, presented a beautiful and illuminating analogy. He cited the 'symbolic notion of fatherhood and motherhood' that has existed in all religions: the Heavenly Father, the Fatherhood of God, the figure of the loving mother in the Virgin, and others. Shoghi Effendi has referred to the nations of the world as 'members of one human family', and Dr Mahmoudi likened 'this great human family' in its present stage of growth to 'the actual institution of the family, with all its needs and requirements to grow and flourish'.

'Love is the most important factor and the essential element of growth and development of the human child,' he said, 'and love is primarily furnished by mother and father . . . or the institutions of motherhood and fatherhood.'

He recalled Erich Fromm's explanation of fatherly love, in *The Art of Loving*, as love based more upon justice; and mother love as a nurturing love, the effects of which are carried throughout adult life.

'The proper amount of motherly and fatherly love', Dr Mahmoudi continued, 'at the proper times when they are needed, bring about and incorporate in the offspring a love which is labeled the "brotherly love" . . . which at its depth is the "love of God", the most fundamental kind of love . . . the love for mankind and the belief in the principle of the unity and the oneness of mankind, which is the foundation and the pivot round which all the teachings of Bahá'u'lláh revolve.'

In another context, within the Bahá'í community, Dr Mahmoudi compares the role of the Spiritual Assembly to that of fatherly guidance and care: 'the loving shepherd of the Bahá'í flock', in the words of the Universal House of Justice. This love reflected by the Spiritual Assembly, based upon justice, is expressed in its ultimate manifestation by the very name these institutions will one day bear: Houses of Justice.

On the other hand the institutions whose functions are

propagation and protection, 'symbolically and character-istically functions of motherhood', are supplementary and complementary to the role of the Spiritual Assembly. But 'no true fatherly love is entirely devoid of motherly love, and vice versa'.

His conclusion: 'It is the cordial cooperation, sincere relationship, understanding, and affectionate interaction and communication between the equally august and loving institutions of fatherhood and motherhood in showing of their love to each other and to each and every Bahá'í individual and community which will guarantee the growth, health and strength of this great world spiritual family and its beloved members.'

Evolution of the Institution of the Counselors

The number of Counselors rose within five years from the original thirty-six to fifty-seven. A five-year term of office was later established and became effective on November 26, 1980, the Day of the Covenant. The scope of their operations now widened to include an entire continent for each expanded Board, to 'accord greater discretion and freedom of action'. The new appointments and re-appointments at that time (November 1980) resulted in the following: Africa — 15; Americas — 16; Asia — 16; Australasia — 7; Europe — 9. Such matters as creating zones of operation within the larger areas, the location of Board offices, and the direction of the Auxiliary Boards, were left to the new Boards of Counselors to work out according to the geographic sphere of their responsibilities.

Every step in the growth and evolvement of the

institutions of Bahá'u'lláh's World Order not only represents signs of its present organic growth but signifies a major opening into the future field of action for the entire community of believers. In announcing this development of the institution of the Counselors, the Universal House of Justice wrote:

Every institution of this divinely created Order is one more refuge for a distraught populace; every soul illumined by the light of the sacred Message is one more link in the oneness of mankind, one more servant ministering to the needs of an ailing world . . . It is our prayer at the Sacred Threshold that the new and challenging development now taking place in the evolution of the institution of the Counselors will release great energies for the advancement of the Cause of God in every land.[50]

In this way do the floodgates of spiritual energy and opportunity open wider to nourish the fountain of the spirit, both individually and collectively.

In this way is the soul transformed from time to time as lives are consecrated anew in the labor of the Kingdom. When the Boards of Counselors convened their first conferences around the world in 1968 a thrilling new motion at work in the Cause was deeply felt by the believers. It was felt again and again as the evolution of this mighty institution created by the House of Justice continued to manifest itself. Within five years of its birth its seal and crown would be visible on the Mountain of God.

7

The International Teaching Center is Formed

The Divine Mystery of God's Holy Mountain

The stately edifice of the Universal House of Justice rises gloriously on the Mountain of God overlooking the resting place of the Greatest Holy Leaf. Close by are entombed her mother, Navváb, and her brother, the Purest Branch. Late in December of 1939 Shoghi Effendi, with tender and agonizing care, had transferred the sacred remains of the mother and brother of 'Abdu'l-Bahá and Báhíyyih Khánum from 'an alien burial-ground' in 'Akká to rest 'within the hallowed precincts' of the Shrine of the Báb. Now all the family of the Master were gathered together in this serene and sacred Spot. In Shoghi Effendi's words, they 'tower in rank above the vast multitude of the heroes, Letters, martyrs, hands, teachers and administrators of the Cause of Bahá'u'lláh . . .' The visit of a Bahá'í to these shrines is less only in its spiritual import to that of pilgrimage to the Shrines of the Central Figures of the Faith.

This act on the part of Shoghi Effendi in creating this

association of these 'incomparably precious souls' had far more than historic or sentimental value. It not only effected a powerful new spiritual dimension in the life of every believer — it was an event, he stated, 'of such capital institutional significance as only future happenings, steadily and mysteriously unfolding at the world center of our Faith, can adequately demonstrate'. Moreover, it 'incalculably reinforces the spiritual potencies of that consecrated Spot which . . . is destined to evolve into the focal center of those world-shaking, world-embracing, world-directing administrative institutions, ordained by Bahá'u'lláh and anticipated by 'Abdu'l-Bahá . . .'[51]

Again, he related these developments at the world center to the Tablet of Carmel and Bahá'u'lláh's words: *'Ere long will God sail His Ark upon thee . . .'*

The Crowning Institution of the Learned

Ten years had elapsed since the 'Ark' had been visibly established upon Carmel with the formation of the Universal House of Justice. Now a cablegram from that august Body flashed around the Bahá'í world on June 5, 1973, echoing the Guardian's premonitory words: 'Announce establishment Holy Land long anticipated International Teaching Center destined evolve into one of those world shaking world embracing world directing administrative institutions ordained by Bahá'u'lláh anticipated by 'Abdu'l-Bahá elucidated by Shoghi Effendi.'

All Hands of the Cause of God, wherever they resided, were named as members of the International Teaching Center, to be informed of its activities, to make suggestions and recommendations to that body, and to participate fully in its deliberations when they were present in the Holy Land.

The working nucleus of this new institution at the world center consisted of the Hands of the Cause present in the Holy Land: Amatu'l-Bahá Rúḥíyyih Khánum, A. Q. Faizi, 'Ali-Akbár Furútan, Paul Haney; and three Counselors appointed to this body: Hooper Dunbar (South America), Florence Mayberry (North America), and 'Azíz Yazdí (Central and East Africa).

The seal was set — the crowning institution of the learned was now established in the Holy Land. In the course of time it would 'operate from that building designated by the Guardian as the Seat for the Hands of the Cause, which must be raised on the arc on Mount Carmel in close proximity to the Seat of the Universal House of Justice.'

An inaugural meeting took place in Baḥjí on June 14 with the Universal House of Justice, and the following duties were assigned:

To coordinate, stimulate and direct the activities of the Continental Boards of Counselors and to act as liaison between them and the Universal House of Justice.

To be fully informed of the situation of the Cause in all parts of the world and to be able, from the background of this knowledge, to make reports and recommendations to the Universal House of Justice and give advice to the Continental Boards of Counselors.

To be alert to possibilities, both within and without the Bahá'í community, for the extension of the teaching work into receptive or needy areas, and to draw the attention of the Universal House of Justice and the Continental Boards of Counselors to such possibilities, making recommendations for action.

To determine and anticipate needs for literature, pioneers and traveling teachers and to work out teaching plans, both regional and global, for the approval of the Universal House of Justice.[52]

Problems concerning Covenant-breaking, investigated locally by the Counselors in consultation with any Hands in the area, would be referred to the Teaching Center where decisions on the matter would be made by the Hands of the Cause residing in the Holy Land, final approval to come from the Universal House of Justice.

With these awesome duties before them, the new institution began its work. Six days after their inauguration their first letter went out to all members of the Continental Boards of Counselors, stating the need for 'a greatly increased flow of vital information from the Counselors, reflecting the situation of the Cause throughout their respective zones . . .' It would be a two-way flow, for paralleling this would be 'the development of an even closer relationship between the Counselors and the Institutions in the Holy Land . . .'[53]

An immediate task before them was to assist the House of Justice in formulating a Five Year Plan to be released at Naw-Rúz 1974. In this Naw-Rúz message to the Bahá'ís of the world the House of Justice confidently expressed its view that the love and guidance of this institution, reflected through its subordinate institutions, now 'permeates the entire structure of Bahá'í society'.

Major Steps in the Evolution of the International Teaching Center

In June of 1973 when the International Teaching Center

was inaugurated there were seventeen Hands of the Cause
of God still living, from the original twenty-seven who had
existed at the time of Shoghi Effendi's passing. Ten years
later there remained ten of these 'most precious assets the
Bahá'í world possesses' — only two residing in the Holy
Land. The wisdom of the gradual extension into the
future of the functions of the Hands of the Cause through
the establishment of the Boards of Counselors and the
International Teaching Center was clearly apparent. Now
in May of 1983 it was time for major new steps to be
taken:

1. Hands of the Cause of God Dr 'Ali-Muḥammad
Varqá and Mr Collis Featherstone were called upon to
discharge special duties of the Hands of the Cause in the
Holy Land (for example, matters of Covenant-breaking)
either by correspondence or periodic visits to the World
Center.

2. The number of resident members of the Teaching
Center was raised to nine with the appointment of Dr
Magdalene Carney, Mr Mas'úd K̲h̲amsí, Dr Peter Khan,
and Mrs Isobel Sabri. (Mrs Florence Mayberry returned
to America for reasons of health; and Counselor Anneliese Bopp of Germany had been appointed to the Center
in July of 1979.)*

3. A five-year term of office was instituted for the Counselor members, beginning May 23 following each
International Bahá'í Convention.

Commensurate with these new developments there
came also an expansion of duties. Being alert to teaching

* The members of the Center now residing in the Holy Land therefore included the
four new appointees above, plus Hands of the Cause Amatu'l-Bahá Rúḥíyyih
K̲h̲ánum, A. Furútan; and Counselors Anneliese Bopp, Hooper Dunbar, and 'Azíz
Yazdí.

opportunities now included 'the development of economic and social life both within and without the Bahá'í community'. Directing the work of the Continental Pioneer Committees; administering the expenditure of the International Deputization Fund; and administering an annual budget (from the Bahá'í International Fund) for special teaching projects, literature subvention, and Continental Funds (when needed) were all added to the responsibilities of this evolving 'world-embracing' institution of the Faith.

How evident it was to every loyal, dedicated Bahá'í that the Divine Charters had once again yielded precious fruit upon the Mountain of God 'in a land which', Shoghi Effendi had written, 'geographically, spiritually and administratively, constitutes the heart of the entire planet . . .'[54]

8

Permeating the Grass Roots: The Auxiliary Boards and their Assistants

What Does an Auxiliary Board Member Do?

It was the last evening of a three-day visit by a member of the Auxiliary Board. Assembly members and about twenty other Bahá'ís had gathered for a last informal discussion. During the three days there had been an all-day institute on the Covenant and the institutions evolving from that Covenant, with special emphasis on the Spiritual Assembly. Between two long sessions with the Assembly (having been invited to come and assist in ironing out some difficulties), the Board member had met individually with each Assembly member. Mornings and afternoons were also filled with individual interviews: a young woman having difficulty understanding the law of parental consent when it applied to parents who were not Bahá'ís; a college student concerned about his own responsibility in respect to a fellow Bahá'í observed drinking on campus; a couple longing to go pioneering abroad but concerned about debts they would not then be able to handle; an elderly believer who was feeling 'left out' of the mainstream of community activity. All these and many others brought their problems, desires and hopes to be talked over objectively, lovingly, with frequent references to the Sacred Writings or to the counsel given by Shoghi Effendi and the Universal House of Justice. Often the comment was made: 'I didn't know that was in the Writings. Where can I find it?'

Now, on this last evening, there was a free and open discussion with many questions being asked.

A hand was raised in the back row: 'Tell me, what does an Auxiliary Board member do?'

There was a gasp or two and then embarrassed silence. Someone said: 'Oh Joe! She's been doing it for three days. Where have you been?'

Joe had indeed been one who had absorbed several hours of the Board member's time seeking advice in sorting out the priorities in his young life.

'It's a good question, Joe,' assured the Board member. 'But before I comment on it I would like to ask those of you here to answer the question.'

There was a brief hesitation, then: 'All I can say', said an Assembly member, 'is that I've gotten for the first time a larger view of what Bahá'í consultation should be, and how wasteful it is when we get so wrapped up in personalities — and in our own ideas.'

'It's been wonderful having someone objective to bounce all of our conceptions and misconceptions against', said another.

The young woman concerned about parental consent spoke up: 'You've cleared away some fuzzy thinking on my part. I've a better concept of what the laws of Bahá'u'lláh mean. I used to look on them as restraints and obstacles to my freedom. Now I see they really give access to freedom — spiritual freedom.'

'Yes,' responded the Board member, 'they are like guideposts along the path of life. It's important to remember what Shoghi Effendi said. It's necessary to have tests and difficulties — they strengthen us, help us grow. He said, "The troubles of this world pass, and what we have left is what we have made of our souls . . ." and Bahá'u'lláh revealed the laws of God to make it easier for us to spiritualize our lives, to "build" our souls, so to speak.'

There was a pause. Then a hand was raised again from the back row, along with some muffled groans. It was Joe again: 'Hey, I know what an Auxiliary Board member is! You are like a good Aunt to us. Parents are like the Assembly and they must be obeyed. But an Aunt has a lot of loving advice and help to give us and it can save us from making so many dumb mistakes.'*

'What a beautiful analogy!' The Board member smiled in appreciation. 'I shall always remember that.'

A Persian youth said: 'In my town in Iran we used to call the Auxiliary Board members our "uncles and aunts" when they came to visit us.'

The Universal House of Justice has summed up the work of the Board members: 'Above all the Auxiliary Board members should build up a warm and loving relationship between themselves and the believers in their area so that the Local Spiritual Assemblies will spontaneously turn to them for advice and assistance.'[55]

* The incident occurred — only the name is changed.

Because this relationship is often on a one-to-one level, the Board member can frequently be a direct channel of loving counsel and support — the aim being to orient the individual believer or Assembly to fullest service in the Cause of God, the only source of true contentment.

The matter of confidentiality enters into the relationship of the individual with his Auxiliary Board member.

If a believer turns to an assistant or Auxiliary Board member for advice on a personal matter it is for the assistant or Auxiliary Board member to decide whether he should advise the believer to turn to his Spiritual Assembly, whether he should himself give advice and, in either case, whether he should report the matter to the Counselors, or to the Local Assembly, which, of course, would depend upon the degree of confidentiality he had undertaken to observe. Likewise, it is for the Counselor to decide whether it is a matter of which the National Assembly should be informed. All this is, of course, within the general context that, apart from matters which ought to remain confidential, the more freely information is shared between the institutions of the Faith the better.[56]

The Board member has the benefit of being able to move freely within the community he serves, talking with individuals, lending assistance in whatever ways he can. The Supreme Body has encouraged not only meeting with the Local Assembly but 'with the local community members, collectively at general meetings and even, if necessary, individually in their homes'.

'Alí Nakhjavání, member of the Universal House of Justice, once said that of all the services he had been privileged to render the Cause during his pioneering years in East and Central Africa, he had most enjoyed serving as an Auxiliary Board member. 'An Auxiliary Board member has a wonderful challenge', he said. 'He has much freedom with which to carry out his work. He himself assesses, for the most part, where he is needed and how to be of the greatest assistance to the believers in both their individual and collective efforts — and can devise his own methods and ways of encouraging, stimulating and inspiring them.'

Although the Counselors should regularly direct the work of the Auxiliary Board members, 'they should give to each Auxiliary Board member considerable freedom of action within his own allocated area'. Board members 'need not wait for direction; the nature of their work is such that they should be continually engaged in it according to their own best judgment . . .'[57]

The 'value of their interaction' resulting from the effective collaboration of the two institutions comes in witnessing, through the grace of Bahá'u'lláh, a change of behavior on the part of an individual who had been heading in a negative direction; a Spiritual Assembly, having growing pains, discovering anew the source of the power that is theirs to draw upon, enabling them to function more effectively; a whole community quickened with a fresh spirit of enthusiasm for teaching the Cause.

'Thus it is seen', the House of Justice has written, 'that the Auxiliary Boards should work closely with the grass roots of the community: the individual believers, groups and Local Spiritual Assemblies, advising, stimulating and assisting them.'[58]

The Grass Roots of the Community

What are the grass roots? Who is a grass roots Bahá'í? We are all grass roots Bahá'ís. The local community is the spiritual and administrative 'home' of each believer. It is where we all fundamentally abide as believers. There is no such thing as a 'national' or 'international' Bahá'í, although individuals serve in varying capacities on these administrative levels wherein their responsibilities encompass these wider spheres of activity in the Administrative Order.

The grass roots, the local community, the foundation of the World Order of Bahá'u'lláh, begins with the planting of the seed of the Word of God. Bursting with the life-force of the Spirit, it sends down roots, where it is nourished and held by the soil of the laws of God upheld by the Spiritual Assembly. Simultaneously it thrusts its shoots skyward toward the sun and rain of the love of God, then blossoms and bears fruit and scatters more seed. The seeds germinate, the roots spread, the community grows.

In one context the work of the Auxiliary Board members and their assistants can be seen as the concerned and loving gardeners of these plants. The Supreme Body expressed its confidence 'that the institution of the Boards of Counselors will lend its vital support and, through the Counselors' own contacts with the friends, through their Auxiliary Boards and their assistants, will nourish the roots of each local community, enrich and cultivate the soil of knowledge of the teachings and irrigate it with the living waters of love for Bahá'u'lláh. Thus will the saplings grow into mighty trees, and the trees bear their golden fruit.'[59]

An Auxiliary Board member does not carry with him a magic fire or perfect knowledge of the Writings. He does bring an objective insight and a disinterested viewpoint on matters that often get hopelessly mixed with personalities in the day-to-day proximity of Assembly work. He also has a commitment to an ongoing study of the Teachings. Above all, he has faith that *all* the institutions of the Faith of Bahá'u'lláh are endowed with a power to fulfill the purpose for which they were raised up.

What Auxiliary Board Members Do Not Do

1. *Adjudicate.* Adjudication means to make a judgment and/or a decision on action to be taken in terms of official warning, sanctions or restrictions of various kinds, including removal of administrative rights, or the regaining of them. Although a Board member may do what he can to advise, counsel and try to avert the necessity of such sanctions, once such matters are turned over to the ruling corporate body for action, the Board member is not involved in the procedures. He does have a role *after* such procedures are taken in assisting the individual believer to reorient his life to the Cause of Bahá'u'lláh, or in educating and strengthening an Assembly.

2. *Administer.* As mentioned in a previous chapter, both Counselors and Auxiliary Board members have a responsibility to advise Assemblies on administrative matters. 'The statement that they do not have anything to do with administration means, simply, that they do not administer. They do not direct or organize the teaching work nor do they adjudicate in matters of personal conflict or personal problems. All these activities fall within the sphere of responsibility of the Spiritual Assemblies,' wrote the House of Justice. An example given is that of a believer

inspired by a Board member to pioneer. He must then be referred to the proper committee. 'Counselors and Auxiliary Board members should not, themselves, organize pioneering or travel teaching projects.'[60]

3. *Legislate.* Although Board members may consult with an Assembly and give advice on various matters requiring legislation, they do not participate in the actual decision-making process. Voting and making decisions on matters rests solely with the Spiritual Assembly.

Thus it is seen that the above functions in all of their ramifications belong exclusively to the ruling, corporate, elected bodies of the Faith.

Expansion of the Institution of the Auxiliary Board

As in the case of the International Teaching Center and the Boards of Counselors, the institution of the Auxiliary Board also evolved through the years both in numbers and in the scope of its responsibilities, reflecting generally the development of the higher institutions directing its work. By October of 1973 the number of Auxiliary Board members throughout the world had increased from its original 36 members to a total of 270, with 81 serving the Protection Board and 189 serving the Propagation Board. This growth in numbers withal, it was yet clear that 'permeating the grass roots' would require other measures. The action came on June 8, 1973 in a letter from the Supreme Body to the Continental Boards of Counselors, later announced 'to the Bahá'ís of the world' on October 7, 1973: 'We have decided to take a further step in the development of this institution and to give to each Continental Board of Counselors the discretion to authorize individual Auxiliary Board members to appoint assistants.'

The appointments were to be made for a period of a year or two with the possibility of re-appointment. Although the International Teaching Center and the Hands of the Cause of God, the Continental Boards of Counselors and the Auxiliary Boards are each an individual institution under the umbrella of 'the learned', the assistants do not form an individual institution but are rather a *part* of the institution of the Auxiliary Board. Thus an assistant is always 'assistant to Auxiliary Board Member John Jones' and not a part of a separate category or institution of 'auxiliary board assistants'. Furthermore, assistants are free to serve on Local Assemblies, as delegates, members of committees and in other administrative duties.*

Their primary functions are 'to activate and encourage Local Spiritual Assemblies, to call the attention of Local Spiritual Assembly members to the importance of holding regular meetings, to encourage local communities to meet for the Nineteen Day Feasts and Holy Days, to help deepen their fellow-believers' understanding of the Teachings and generally to assist the Auxiliary Board members in the discharge of their duties'.

This expansion of the Auxiliary Board at the grass roots level gave the Board members increased awareness of and closeness to the needs of the believers in their areas of service. There were practical economic benefits also derived from this focus on a smaller, localized geographic area, as well as in the possibility of increasing the number of assistants quickly as the need arose.

---

* The Constitution of the Universal House of Justice states that although an Auxiliary Board member is eligible for any elective office, he must, if elected to an administrative post on a national or local level, 'decide whether to retain membership on the Board or accept the administrative post, since he may not serve in both capacities at the same time'.

Two Boards with Distinct but Complementary Functions

Shoghi Effendi did not specify in great detail how the Auxiliary Board would function, leaving this to be worked out in the light of experience. In his last message of October 1957 he had called for an additional and separate Board 'charged with the specific duty of watching over the security of the Faith'. While each Board member had a specific territory to serve, the Protection Board members, for a period of time, served additionally as the need arose in any locality and as called upon by the Hands of the Cause and later the Counselors.

Article X of the Constitution of the Universal House of Justice reads: 'In each zone there shall be two Auxiliary Boards, one for the protection and one for the propagation of the Faith.' In 1976 the Supreme Body, through the International Teaching Center, asked the Counselors to implement this allocation of Board members, one each of the two Boards, Protection and Propagation, for each area or zone. Thus all areas had both a Protection and Propagation Board member assigned to them to whom they could refer and who in turn served them.

Watching Over the Security of the Faith

In elucidating the functions of the Protection Board, the Universal House of Justice wrote:

The need to protect the Faith from the attacks of its enemies is not generally appreciated by the friends . . . However, we know that these attacks will increase and will become concerted and universal. The writings of our Faith clearly foreshadow not only an intensification of the machinations of internal enemies, but a rise in the hostility and opposition of its external enemies, whether religious or secular, as our beloved Faith pursues its onward march towards ultimate victory.

And again,

Above all, the members of the Protection Boards should concentrate on deepening the friends' knowledge of the Covenant and increasing their love and loyalty to it, on clearly and frankly answering, in conformity with the teachings, whatever questions may trouble any of the believers, on fostering the spiritual profundity and strength of their Faith and certitude, and on promoting whatever will increase the spirit of loving unity in Bahá'í communities.[61]

The International Teaching Center summarized its view that 'protection of the Faith involves preservation of the spiritual health of the individual believers and communities, as well as specialized protection activities relative to the Covenant'.

Standard-bearers of the Teachers of the Faith

'The primary tasks of the Propagation Boards, however, are to direct the believers' attention to the goals of whatever plans have been placed before them, to stimulate and assist them to promote the teaching work in the fields of proclamation, expansion, consolidation and pioneering, to encourage contributions to the funds, and to act as standard-bearers of the teachers of the Faith, leading them to new achievements in the diffusion of God's Message to their fellow human beings.' This statement from the House of Justice was augmented by the following letter of September 29, 1976, from the International Teaching Center: 'The Propagation Board members will become more precisely involved in the attainment of the Five Year Plan goals. This follows the indication relative to the distinction between services given by the Guardian in his establishment of the additional Board when he stated that the Propagation Board members would "henceforth be exclusively concerned with assisting the prosecution of the Ten Year Crusade Plan".'

As to the question of how Local Assemblies and individual believers would know which matters they should refer to which Auxiliary Board member, the House of Justice stated that they 'should not concern themselves unduly about it . . . They should feel free to refer to either Board, and if the Auxiliary Board member feels that the matter would better have been referred to his colleague, he can either himself pass the question on, or suggest the different approach to the Assembly or believer.'[62]

The Auxiliary Board — A Volunteer Service

Someone once asked at a conference: 'How do you apply to be an Auxiliary Board member?' This was followed by laughter, but it is understandable that new believers especially may not be apprised of the way in which the institutions of the Faith carry on their work. The Auxiliary Board is strictly an appointed, volunteer service. The Board members have no staff, no office or equipment other than what they can provide for themselves, and all their work, the volume of correspondence and reports and other activities, devolves upon themselves at this stage of the institution's development — with the assistants carrying out their supportive work in the field. There are no salaries involved, though the members are entitled to reimbursement for traveling and other out-of-pocket expenses. A Board member is primarily a teacher of the Cause, and, as pointed out in an earlier chapter, the qualities and functions are shared by all teachers and promoters of the Cause, the difference being that a Board member has an ongoing and constant responsibility toward the believers in his given area.

The Individual Bahá'í — Seizing the Initiative

'The heart of the Guardian cannot but leap with joy', wrote Shoghi Effendi as the great World Crusade got underway, '. . . at every evidence testifying to the response of the individual to his allotted task.'[63]

And the Universal House of Justice has emphasized that although authority and direction as well as inspiration and protection flow from institutions, 'the power to accomplish the tasks resides primarily in the entire body of believers'.[64]

The individual believer and his initiatory rise to action is the spark that ignites the fuel and moves the entire machinery of the Cause. 'Without his support, at once whole-hearted, continuous, generous, every measure adopted and every plan formulated . . . is doomed to failure', observed the Guardian. The challenge rests upon the 'individual believer, on whom in the last resort depends the fate of the entire community. He . . . constitutes the warp and woof on which the quality and pattern of the whole fabric must depend. He . . . acts as one of the countless links in the mighty chain that now girdles the globe.'[65]

The human body grows to maturity through the action

of individual cells, combining and fulfilling their potential within the greater structure of the body. The Faith grows through the action of individual Bahá'ís, joining hands with their fellow Bahá'ís to fulfill their destiny, but not as blind communal lumps.

The Cause of God reflects balance: '... mercy and justice' as well as 'freedom and submission ... the sanctity of the right of the individual and of self-surrender ... vigilance, discretion and prudence on the one hand, and fellowship, candor and courage on the other ...'[66] All these are tentpoles upholding the canopy of unity within the great community of Bahá'ís.

The Guardian stressed in many ways the need to encourage personal initiative on the part of the individual believer. 'Let us also remember', he warned, 'that at the very root of the Cause lies the principle of the undoubted right of the individual to self-expression, his freedom to declare his conscience and set forth his views ... Let us also bear in mind that the keynote of the Cause of God is not dictatorial authority but humble fellowship, not arbitrary power, but the spirit of frank and loving consultation.'[67]

Again, he stated: '... we should not restrict the liberty of the individual to express his own views so long as he makes it clear that these views are his own ... God has given man a rational power to be used and not killed.'

But this principle cannot be abused within the context of the Teachings, for 'absolute authority' must 'remain in the revealed Words. We should try and keep as near to the authority as we can and show that we are faithful to it by quoting from the Words of Bahá'u'lláh in establishing our points.'[68]

In the area of teaching especially is the individual called to act. 'Having on his own initiative, and undaunted by any hindrances with which either friend or foe may, unwittingly or deliberately, obstruct his path, resolved to arise and respond to the call of teaching, let him carefully consider every avenue of approach . . .' These words and many more on this theme were expressed by Shoghi Effendi in his message *The Advent of Divine Justice*. This was released just as the Divine Plan had at last been launched in a formal, organized way in the First Seven Year Plan, and it is a guiding light for every teacher and pioneer, now and for the future, as it was then.

A Bahá'í must also take the initiative in choosing the path his life will take, in developing the spiritual qualities that form his character which are the only powers to be carried into the next world. How to attain such a victory over self is clearly outlined in the compilation prepared for us by the Universal House of Justice entitled *The Bahá'í Life.* * In it we read, 'The individual alone must . . . struggle against the natural inertia that weighs him down.' It is all a vital part of living a Bahá'í life, of 'fighting one's own spiritual battles' as the Supreme Body so lovingly counsels us. The institutions are here, like loving parents, teachers, friends, to guide us safely over our 'bridge of al-Ṣiráṭ' but the key to success rests upon the individual Bahá'í at the *grass roots* of the Cause, that fundamental, strategic foundation of the Bahá'í community. 'The World Center of the Faith itself is paralyzed if such a support on the part of the rank and file of the community is denied it.'[69]

---

* Published in the United Kingdom as *Living the Life*.

9

The Interdependence of Rulers and Learned — A Summing Up

Spiritual Health and Assurance

The believers do not exist for the purpose of creating institutions. The institutions exist to serve the well-being of the Bahá'í community, indeed the whole world. Shoghi Effendi wrote: 'The friends must never mistake the Bahá'í administration for an end in itself. It is merely the instrument of the spirit of the Faith. This Cause is a Cause which God has revealed to humanity as a whole. It is designed to benefit the entire human race . . .'[70] Likewise the degree to which the individual believer relates to the institutions, understands, obeys and supports them, determines the spiritual health of the individual and the entire community which then becomes the key to the regeneration of all mankind.

The Universal House of Justice in their message of September 1964, published under the title of 'Universal Participation', gave a graphic definition of the manner in which all elements in the Faith must interact in order to create a true Bahá'í society. They likened the Bahá'í community to the human body, wherein 'every cell, every organ, every nerve has its part to play. When all do so the body is healthy, vigorous, radiant, ready for every call made upon it. No cell, however humble, lives apart from the body, whether in serving it or receiving from it.'

And 'the Bahá'í world community growing like a healthy new body, develops new cells, new organs, new functions and powers as it presses on to its maturity, when every soul, living for the Cause of God, will receive from the Cause, health, assurance, and the overflowing bounties of Bahá'u'lláh which are diffused through His divinely ordained Order'.[71]

Spiritual health and assurance, therefore, are the birthright of every loyal servant of Bahá'u'lláh! But this certitude comes only to the degree that the individual develops and gives of his own qualities and potential, as well as receives — the extent also to which he relates to those organs of the Faith that have arisen and evolved as the institutions of 'His divinely ordained Order'. Equally vital is the manner in which these institutions relate to each other, particularly the two arms of the Administrative Order known as the 'rulers' and 'learned'. They are as two eyes, two ears, two limbs to the body of the Cause, their correlated effect far greater than the sum of their parts.

A New and Unique Concept

It is clear that the corporate bodies, local and national, direct and administrate the affairs of the Faith at their respective levels, 'revolving around one expressly-designated Pivot': the Universal House of Justice. Manifestly apparent in the operation of all institutions of the 'rulers' and relative to their power and authority is the feature that no individual has any authority of himself but rather only within the consultative power of the institution as a whole.

In Dispensations of the past, ecclesiastical law, administration, interpretation — all facets of religion — came into the province of individuals of various hierarchical rank. Through what were often their 'unyielding and dictatorial views', religious communities fell into a maelstrom of contention, disunity and schism, leading to violence and wars. It is this ruling authority that Bahá'u'lláh has placed in the hands of corporate, elected bodies. And in the words of Shoghi Effendi, 'He has brought all the assemblies together under the shadow of one House of Justice, one divinely-appointed Center . . . making them all proof against schism and division.'[72]

But although Bahá'u'lláh dismissed the authority that once resided primarily in the 'learned', He

nevertheless embodied in His Administrative Order the beneficent elements which exist in such institutions, elements which are of fundamental value for the progress of the Cause . . .

The existence of institutions of such exalted rank, comprising individuals who play such a vital role, who yet have no legislative, administrative or judicial authority, and are entirely devoid of priestly functions or the right to make authoritative interpretations, is a feature of Bahá'í administration unparalleled in the religions of the past. The newness and uniqueness of this concept make it difficult to grasp; only as the Bahá'í Community grows and the believers are increasingly able to contemplate its administrative structure uninfluenced by concepts from past ages, will the vital interdependence of the 'rulers' and 'learned' in the Faith be properly understood, and the inestimable value of their interaction be fully recognized.[73]

As the individual believer is increasingly able to visu-
alize the Faith of Bahá'u'lláh and His Administrative
Order outside of concepts from the past, so will his efforts
augment the rise of His institutions to their place of 'influence and honor'. Conversely, lack of vision, which is
perhaps another word for faith, can prevent the individual
from functioning in harmony and joy within the
framework of that Order.

'The Administrative Order', Shoghi Effendi stated, '. . .
is, by virtue of its origin and character, unique in the
annals of the world's religious systems.'[74]

Its origin? '. . . those hidden springs of celestial strength
which no force of human personality, whatever its glamor,
can replace . . . its reliance is solely upon that mystic
Source with which no worldly advantage, be it wealth,
fame, or learning can compare . . . it propagates itself by
ways mysterious and utterly at variance with the stan-
dards accepted by the generality of mankind . . .'[75]

God's will, revealed through His Manifestation,
Bahá'u'lláh, has given birth to the divine institutions of
His World Order. This Order alone is endowed with the
capacity to usher in the Kingdom of God on earth: that
peaceful world society that has so long occupied
humanity's dreams. It is 'destined to embrace in the fullness of time the whole of mankind'.

Inside a Navajo Indian hogan on a snowy, starlit, Arizona
night, a young assistant to the Auxiliary Board, himself a
Navajo, struggled to convey to his listeners some idea of
the simplicity as well as grandeur of the Administrative
Order of the Faith of Bahá'u'lláh. By the light of a flick-
ering lantern he drew a map of the world, placed dots

upon it for Local Assemblies and connected them to larger dots that represented National Assemblies. These in turn were connected to a large star that was the World Center in the Holy Land.

'That', he said, 'is what holds the world together!'

What could be added to the picture is a kind of candle-light glow, a circle of warmth surrounding each dot, large and small, to represent 'the love, the guidance, the assistance of the Hands, through the Boards of Counselors, their Auxiliary Board members and their assistants' that 'permeates the entire structure of Bahá'í society'.[76]

Fulfillers of the Dream

Members of the Bahá'í world community possess the greatest gift and have been granted, through their faith in Bahá'u'lláh, the most unique and glorious privilege ever given to humanity: to become the instrument for making those dreams a reality. Although as the Master said 'all the forces of the universe . . . serve the Covenant', it is only the believers who are quickened with the divine fire of God's Word for this Day — to them is given the privilege to rekindle the spark of faith in others. That divine fire can only be kept aflame through earnest prayer, deep study of the Word, obedience to the laws, and dedicated effort in spreading His Faith and building the Administrative Order, the vessel that draws from those 'hidden springs', unsullied by interpretations and ideas of the past.

In recent months and years the *'march of the institutions of His world-redeeming Order . . . hastening the estab-*lishment of His Kingdom in the hearts of men' has accelerated swiftly before our eyes. They are challenging us, as mentioned before, 'to stretch mind and spirit' to keep apace. There is a popular vernacularism, usually associated with superficial or trivial fads of the day, that urges us to stay 'with it'. But staying 'with it' in the developments of the Faith of Bahá'u'lláh is our spiritual lifeline and to do so we need to study diligently the messages and directives that flow to us from the Universal House of Justice in the Holy Land. The Plans that they create are our personal Charter. Accepting our part in those Plans is our key to being a 'healthy cell'.

The Bahá'í community is still in its springtime years. It is like a tender plant. It must have its roots firmly held in place; but the illumination and warmth of the sun is also needed. So might we consider the two arms of the Administrative Order that have grown out of the Covenant of Bahá'u'lláh and the institutions they characterize. So will 'the vital interdependence of the "rulers" and "learned" in the Faith' be enabled to yield the 'inestimable value of their interaction'. As our efforts evolve and coalesce so will a joyful awareness permeate the hearts of believers everywhere of the potential for expanding the perimeters of unity that bind together the community of the Most Great Name.

'Blessed are the rulers and the learned among the people of Bahá. They are My trustees among My servants and the manifestations of My commandments amidst My people.'

Appendix

**Hands of the Cause of God appointed by Shoghi Effendi
not including posthumous appointments**

First Contingent, December 24, 1951 †
    Dorothy B. Baker*
    Amelia E. Collins*
    'Alí-Akbar Furútan
    Ugo Giachery
    Hermann Grossmann*
    Horace Holley*
    Leroy Ioas*
    William Sutherland Maxwell*
    Tarázu'lláh Samandarí*
    George Townshend*
    Valíyu'lláh Varqá*

Second Contingent, February 29, 1952
    Shu'á'u'lláh 'Alá'í
    Músá Banání*
    Clara Dunn*
    Dhikru'lláh Khádem
    Adelbert Mühlschlegel*
    Siegfried Schopflocher*
    Corinne True*

*deceased
† Mason Remey, appointed a Hand of the Cause of God in the first contingent, defected in 1960 through a claim to be the 'hereditary Guardian'.

Appointed Singly

Amatu'l-Bahá Rúḥíyyih Khánum (March 26, 1952)

Jalál Kházeh (December 7, 1953)

Paul E. Haney* (March 19, 1954)

'Ali-Muhammad Varqá (November 15, 1955)

Agnes B. Alexander* (March 27, 1957)

Final Contingent, October, 1957

Enoch Olinga*

William Sears

Ḥasan M. Balyuzi*

John Robarts

John Ferraby*

H. Collis Featherstone

Raḥmatu'lláh Muhájir*

Abu'l-Qásim Faizi*

* deceased

The first thirty-six Auxiliary Board members appointed by the Hands of the Cause of God at Riḍván, 1954

Africa: John Allen, Elsie Austin, Muḥammad Muṣṭaphá Soleiman, 'Alí Nakhjavání, Jalál Nakhjavání, John Robarts, William Sears, Valerie Wilson, 'Azíz Yazdí.

America: Esteban Canales, Rowland Estall, William de Forge, Florence Mayberry, Margery McCormick, Katherine McLaughlin, Sarah Pereira, Gayle Woolson, Margot Worley.

Asia: Agnes Alexander, Abbas Ali Butt, Abu'l-Qásim Faizi, Elena Marsella (Fernie), Kazim Kazimzadeh, Carl Scherer, Daoud Toeg.

Europe: Tove Deleuran, Dorothy Ferraby, Angeline Giachery, Anna Grossmann, Louis Hénuzet, Marion Hofman, Eugen Schmidt, Elsa Steinmetz.*

Australasia: H. C. Featherstone, Thelma Perks.

* Joel Marangella became a Covenant-breaker under Mason Remey.

Members of the first historic Universal House of Justice elected at Riḍván, 1963

Charles Wolcott
'Alí Nakhjavání
H. Borrah Kavelin
Ian Semple
Lutfulláh Ḥakím
David Hofman
Hugh Chance
Amoz Gibson
Hushmand Fatheazam

**The first twelve National Spiritual Assemblies formed
from 1923 to 1953**
whose combined efforts launched the Ten Year World
Crusade in 1953 under the guidance of Shoghi Effendi

Australia and New Zealand
British Isles
Canada
Central America
Egypt and Sudan
Germany and Austria
India, Pakistan and Burma
'Iraq
Italy and Switzerland
Persia
South America
United States of America

Note: By the close of the Ten Year Crusade, Riḍván 1963, the prescribed goal of 48
National Spiritual Assemblies had reached 56; by Riḍván 1983, 135 were formed.

The first Continental Boards of Counselors, 1968

Northwestern Africa: Husayn Ardikání,* Muḥammad Kebdani, William Maxwell.

Central and East Africa: Oloro Epyeru, Kolonario Oule, Isobel Sabri, Mihdi Samandarí, 'Azíz Yazdí.*

Southern Africa: Seewoosumbur-Jeehoba Appa, S͟hídán Fatḥ-i-A'ẓam,* Bahiyyih Ford.

North America: Lloyd Gardner, Florence Mayberry, Edna True.*

Central America: Carmen de Burafato, Artemus Lamb, Alfred Osborne.*

South America: Athos Costas, Hooper Dunbar,* Donald Witzel.

Western Asia: Masíḥ Farhangí, Mas'úd K͟hamsí, Hádí Raḥmání,* Manúc͟hihr Salmánpúr, Sankaran-Nair Vasudevan.

Southeast Asia: Yan Kee Leong, K͟hudárahm Paymán,* Chellie Sundram.

Northeast Asia: Rúḥu'lláh Mumtází,* Vicente Samaniego.

Australasia: Suhayl 'Alá'í, Howard Harwood, Thelma Perks.*

Europe: Erik Blumenthal, Dorothy Ferraby,* Louis Hénuzet.

* Trustee, Continental Fund.

References

1. The Universal House of Justice, *Messages from the Universal House of Justice, 1968—1973* (Wilmette, Ill.: Bahá'í Publishing Trust, 1976), p. 95.
2. *Selections from the Writings of 'Abdu'l-Bahá* (Haifa: Bahá'í World Centre, 1978), p. 84.
3. Shoghi Effendi, *The World Order of Bahá'u'lláh* (Wilmette, Ill.: Bahá'í Publishing Trust, 1955) p. 206.
4. Shoghi Effendi, *The Promised Day Is Come* (Wilmette, Ill.: Bahá'í Publishing Trust, 1961), p. 128.
5. The Universal House of Justice, *Wellspring of Guidance* (Wilmette, Ill.: Bahá'í Publishing Trust, 1969), p. 96.
6. *The Bahá'í World: An International Record, Vol. XV, 1968—1973* (Haifa: Bahá'í World Centre, 1976), pp. 621—8.
7. *The Local Spiritual Assembly: An Institution of the Bahá'í Administrative Order*. Compiled by The Universal House of Justice, 1970 (Wilmette, Ill.: Bahá'í Publishing Trust), p. 13.
8. ibid. p. 14.
9. ibid. p. 12.
10. ibid.
11. ibid. p. 17.
12. ibid. p. 9.
13. ibid. p. 24.
14. *Bahá'í Procedure* (Wilmette, Ill.: Bahá'í Publishing Trust, 1942), p. 8.
15. The Universal House of Justice, Message to the Bahá'ís of the World, Naw-Rúz 1974, published in *Bahá'í News*, April 1974.

16. Shoghi Effendi, *Messages to the Bahá'í World: 1950—1957*, rev. edn. (Wilmette, Ill.: Bahá'í Publishing Trust, 1971), p. 8.

17. *Tablets of Bahá'u'lláh* (Haifa: Bahá'í World Centre, 1978), p. 83.

18. Shoghi Effendi, *Messages to the Bahá'í World*, p. 14.

19. ibid. pp. 122—3.

20. ibid. p. 127.

21. 'Abdu'l-Bahá, *The Secret of Divine Civilization* (Wilmette, Ill.: Bahá'í Publishing Trust, 1957), p. 40.

22. Shoghi Effendi, *Messages to the Bahá'í World*, p. 130.

23. Rúḥíyyih Rabbani, *The Priceless Pearl* (London: Bahá'í Publishing Trust, 1969), p. 443.

24. Proclamation by the Hands of the Cause to the Bahá'ís of East and West, 'Akká, November 25, 1957, published in *Bahá'í News*, January 1958.

25. *The Promulgation of Universal Peace: Talks Delivered by 'Abdu'l-Bahá during His Visit to the United States and Canada in 1912*, rev. edn. (Wilmette, Ill.: Bahá'í Publishing Trust, 1982), p. 455.

26. ibid.

27. *Tablets of Bahá'u'lláh* (Kitáb-i-'Ahd), p. 221.

28. *Selections from the Writings of 'Abdu'l-Bahá*, p. 212.

29. Rúḥíyyih Rabbani, *The Priceless Pearl*, p. 118.

30. *Star of the West.* The Bahá'í Magazine, Vol. X, p. 246.

31. ibid. p. 236.

32. Letter from Shoghi Effendi through his secretary to the National Spiritual Assembly of the United States, published in *Bahá'í News*, June 1949, p. 2.

33. *Will and Testament of 'Abdu'l-Bahá* (Wilmette, Ill.: Bahá'í Publishing Trust, 1968), pp. 18—19.

34. Letter from Shoghi Effendi to an Individual, in *Bahá'í News*, January 1946, p. 1.

35. *Selections from the Writings of 'Abdu'l-Bahá*, pp. 208—9.

36. The Universal House of Justice, *Wellspring of Guidance*, p. 4.

37. ibid. p. 52.

38. ibid. pp. 84—5. (Quoting 'Abdu'l-Bahá.)

39. *Messages from the Universal House of Justice, 1968–1973*, p. 42.

40. ibid. pp. 40–41.

41. Shoghi Effendi, *Unfolding Destiny: The Messages from the Guardian of the Bahá'í Faith to the Bahá'í Community of the British Isles* (London: Bahá'í Publishing Trust, 1981), p. 261.

42. The Universal House of Justice, *Wellspring of Guidance*, p. 41.

43. ibid. p. 42.

44. ibid. pp. 141–2.

45. The Universal House of Justice, *Further Development of Continental Boards of Counsellors, November 3, 1980*, addressed to the Bahá'ís of the World, also published in *The Continental Boards of Counsellors: Letters, Extracts from Letters, and Cables from the Universal House of Justice* (Wilmette, Ill.: Bahá'í Publishing Trust, 1981), p. 67.

46. *Messages from the Universal House of Justice, 1968–1973*, pp. 30–31.

47. ibid. p. 32.

48. *The Continental Boards of Counsellors: Letters*, etc., p. 59.

49. *Messages from the Universal House of Justice, 1968–1973*, pp. 92, 94.

50. The Universal House of Justice, Message to the Bahá'ís of the World, November 3, 1980.

51. Shoghi Effendi, *Messages to America*, Chapter entitled 'The Spiritual Potencies of That Consecrated Spot' (Wilmette, Ill.: Bahá'í Publishing Committee, 1947), pp. 31–3.

52. *Bahá'í News*, cable and letter from the Universal House of Justice to the Bahá'ís of the World, August 1973.

53. International Teaching Center, letter to the Members of all Continental Boards of Counselors, June 20, 1973.

54. Shoghi Effendi, *Messages to America*, p. 33.

55. *Messages from the Universal House of Justice, 1968–1973*, p. 33.

56. Letter to the National Spiritual Assembly of the Virgin Islands, August 2, 1982.

57. *Messages from the Universal House of Justice, 1968–1973*, p. 33.

58. ibid. p. 30.
59. Letter from The Universal House of Justice to all National Spiritual Assemblies, May 25, 1975.
60. *Messages from the Universal House of Justice, 1968—1973*, pp. 32, 30.
61. Letter from the International Teaching Center to the Continental Boards of Counselors, citing instructions from The Universal House of Justice, October 14, 1976.
62. ibid.
63. Shoghi Effendi, *Citadel of Faith* (Wilmette, Ill.: Bahá'í Publishing Trust, 1965), p. 131.
64. *Messages from the Universal House of Justice, 1968—1973*, p. 30.
65. *Citadel of Faith*, p. 130.
66. Shoghi Effendi, *Bahá'í Administration* (Wilmette, Ill.: Bahá'í Publishing Trust, 1969), p. 64.
67. ibid. p. 63.
68. Shoghi Effendi in *Bahá'í Procedure*, compiled by the National Spiritual Assembly of the Bahá'ís of the U.S. and Canada (Wilmette, Ill.: Bahá'í Publishing Committee, 2nd edn. 1942), pp. 17—18.
69. *Citadel of Faith*, p. 131.
70. *The Local Spiritual Assembly*, pp. 28, 29.
71. The Universal House of Justice, *Wellspring of Guidance*, pp. 37—8.
72. *Messages from the Universal House of Justice, 1968—1973*, p. 95.
73. ibid.
74. Shoghi Effendi, *God Passes By* (Wilmette, Ill.: Bahá'í Publishing Trust, 1970), p. 326.
75. Shoghi Effendi, 'The Golden Age of the Cause of Bahá'u'lláh', published in the compilation *The World Order of Bahá'u'lláh* (Wilmette, Ill.: Bahá'í Publishing Trust, 1955), p. 51.
76. The Universal House of Justice, Message to the Bahá'ís of the World launching the Five Year Plan, Naw-Ruz 1974, published in *Bahá'í News*, April 1974.

Books for Further Reading

Bahá'í Scripture and Basic Texts

BAHÁ'U'LLÁH. *Tablets of Bahá'u'lláh*. Compiled by the Universal House of Justice, 1978. Trans. by Habib Taherzadeh and Committee. Haifa: Bahá'í World Centre, 1978.

—— *Gleanings from the Writings of Bahá'u'lláh*. Trans. by Shoghi Effendi. Wilmette, Ill.: Bahá'í Publishing Trust, 2nd rev. edn. 1976.

—— *The Proclamation of Bahá'u'lláh*. Tablets addressed to the kings and leaders of the world. Haifa: Bahá'í World Centre, 1967.

'ABDU'L-BAHÁ. *Selections from the Writings of 'Abdu'l-Bahá*. Compiled by the Research Department of the Universal House of Justice. Haifa: Bahá'í World Centre, 1978.

—— *Foundations of World Unity*. Wilmette, Ill.: Bahá'í Publishing Trust, 1971.

—— *Some Answered Questions*. A series of table talks on a wide variety of topics. Wilmette, Ill.: Bahá'í Publishing Trust, 5th edn. 1981.

—— *The Promulgation of Universal Peace*: Talks Delivered by 'Abdu'l-Bahá during His Visit to the United States and Canada in 1912. Wilmette, Ill.: Bahá'í Publishing Trust, 2nd edn. 1982.

—— *The Secret of Divine Civilization*. A message to the rulers and people of Persia which applies to the general state of modern civilization. Intro. by Horace Holley. Trans. by Marzieh Gail. Wilmette, Ill.: Bahá'í Publishing Trust, 1957.

SHOGHI EFFENDI. *The Advent of Divine Justice.* Preface by Hand of the Cause Paul Haney. Prerequisites for teaching, and living a Bahá'í life. Wilmette, Ill.: Bahá'í Publishing Trust, 3rd edn. 1969.

—— *Bahá'í Administration.* Selected Messages, 1922–1932. Foundation principles for establishing Bahá'í institutions. Wilmette, Ill.: Bahá'í Publishing Trust, 1969.

—— *Citadel of Faith.* Messages to America, 1947–1957. Preface by Paul Haney. Wilmette, Ill.: Bahá'í Publishing Trust, 1965.

—— *God Passes By.* Historical review of first Bahá'í century, 1844–1944. Wilmette, Ill.: Bahá'í Publishing Trust, 6th printing, 1970.

—— *Call to the Nations.* Extracts from statements on world order. Haifa: Bahá'í World Centre, 1977.

—— *Messages to the Bahá'í World: 1950–1957.* Intro. by Horace Holley. Wilmette, Ill.: Bahá'í Publishing Trust, 1971.

—— *The Promised Day Is Come.* A commentary on Bahá'u'lláh's Tablets to the rulers, and present moral and social chaos of the world. Wilmette, Ill.: Bahá'í Publishing Trust, rev. edn. 1980.

—— *Light of Divine Guidance.* Messages from the Guardian of the Bahá'í Faith to Germany and Austria (in English). Hofheim-Langenhain: Bahá'í-Verlag, 1983.

—— *Unfolding Destiny.* Messages from Shoghi Effendi to the Bahá'í Community of the British Isles. Preface by David Hofman. Intro. by Philip Hainsworth. A monumental collection from 1922 to 1957. London: Bahá'í Publishing Trust, 1981.

—— *The World Order of Bahá'u'lláh.* Intro. and Preface by Horace Holley. Seven letters on the theme of world order: 'America and the Most Great Peace'; 'The Goal of a New World Order'; 'The Unfoldment of World Civilization'; 'The Dispensation of Bahá'u'lláh' and others. Wilmette, Ill.: Bahá'í Publishing Trust, 1965.

Note: In addition to those listed above, collections of messages from Shoghi Effendi to various national communities have been published, including: Alaska (*High Endeavours*); Canada (*Messages to Canada*); Australia and New Zealand (*Letters from the Guardian to Australia and New Zealand 1923–1957*); India (*Dawn of a New Day*); New Zealand (*Arohanui*).

THE UNIVERSAL HOUSE OF JUSTICE. *The Continental Boards of Counselors: Letters, Extracts from Letters, and Cables from the Universal House of Justice.* Wilmette, Ill.: Bahá'í Publishing Trust, 1981.

Biographies of the three Central Figures of the Bahá'í Faith and the Guardian

BALYUZI, H. M. *Bahá'u'lláh, the King of Glory.* Oxford: George Ronald, 1980.
—— *The Báb, The Herald of the Day of Days.* Oxford: George Ronald, 1974.
—— *'Abdu'l-Bahá, The Centre of the Covenant of Bahá'u'lláh.* Oxford: George Ronald, 1973.
RABBANÍ, RÚḤÍYYIH. *The Priceless Pearl.* The Life of Shoghi Effendi. London: Bahá'í Publishing Trust, 1969.

The Bahá'í World Volumes: An International Record
Compiled by Shoghi Effendi (I-XII) and by the Universal House of Justice (XIII-). Vols I-XVIII, 1925 to 1980. Wilmette, Ill.: Bahá'í Publishing Trust, RP 1981. *Compendium of Volumes I-XII.* Contains most important features of first twelve volumes. Oxford: George Ronald, 1981.

Introductory Books and Commentaries

BRAUN, EUNICE. *A Crown of Beauty.* The Bahá'í Faith and the Holy Land. Oxford: George Ronald, 1982.
—— *From Strength to Strength.* A Half Century of the Formative Age of the Bahá'í Faith. Wilmette, Ill.: Bahá'í Publishing Trust, 1978.
ESSLEMONT, J. E. *Bahá'u'lláh and the New Era.* History and

teachings of the Bahá'í Faith, available in many languages. Wilmette, Ill.: Bahá'í Publishing Trust, 4th rev. edn. 1975.

HOFMAN, DAVID. *The Renewal of Civilization.* Brief account of history and teachings. Oxford: George Ronald, 1981.

—— *George Townshend.* Biography of one of the finest Bahá'í writers who at one time was Canon of St. Patrick's Cathedral, Dublin, and Archdeacon of Clonfert. Oxford: George Ronald, 1983.

HOLLEY, HORACE. *Religion for Mankind.* Essays on world religion as the progenitor of world order and world peace. Oxford: George Ronald, 1976.

HUDDLESTON, JOHN. *The Earth is But One Country.* A very complete analysis of the needs of mankind today and the contribution of the Bahá'í Faith to the development of world peace and a world-wide civilization. London: Bahá'í Publishing Trust, 1976.

MOMEN, MOOJAN (ed.). *Studies in Bábí and Bahá'í History.* Vol. 1. Three of the five essays analyse aspects of the development in the U.S. of the Bahá'í Administrative Order. Los Angeles: Kalimát Press, 1982.

SCHAEFER, UDO. *The Imperishable Dominion.* The Bahá'í Faith and the Future of Mankind. Trans. from the German. Intro. by Dr. Jacques Chouleur, prof. at the University of Avignon, France. Analysis of the spiritual solutions offered by the Bahá'í Faith as the remedy for the moral crisis and social upheaval of today's world. Oxford: George Ronald, 1983.

TAHERZADEH, ADIB. *The Revelation of Bahá'u'lláh.* Vol. 1: Baghdád 1853-63; Vol. 2: Adrianople 1863-68; Vol. 3: 'Akká, The Early Years 1868-77. Oxford: George Ronald, 1974, 1977, 1983. A survey of the Writings of the Founder of the Bahá'í Faith set in their historical context.

TOWNSHEND, GEORGE. *Christ and Bahá'u'lláh; The Heart of the Gospel; The Promise of All Ages.* Three books with special significance to Christianity. Oxford: George Ronald, RP 1983.